Tressa

Tressa Middleton and Katy Weitz

Tressa
The 12-Year-Old Mum

My True Story

JOHN BLAKE

Published by John Blake Publishing Ltd,
3 Bramber Court, 2 Bramber Road,
London W14 9PB, England

www.johnblakepublishing.co.uk

www.facebook.com/johnblakebooks ⬛
twitter.com/jblakebooks ⬛

This edition published in 2015

ISBN: 978 1 78418 376 9

British Library Cataloguing-in-Publication Data:

A catalogue record for this book is available from the British Library.

Design by www.envydesign.co.uk

Printed in Great Britain by CPI Group (UK) Ltd

3 5 7 9 10 8 6 4 2

Papers used by John Blake Publishing are natural, recyclable products
made from wood grown in sustainable forests. The manufacturing processes
conform to the environmental regulations of the country of origin.

Every attempt has been made to contact the relevant copyright-holders,
but some were unobtainable. We would be grateful if the appropriate
people could contact us.

This book is dedicated to my little girl Annie.
I love you with all my heart and always will.
My life will be complete the day I meet
my sweet baby once again.

Some say the world will end in fire,
Some say in ice.
From what I've tasted of desire
I hold with those who favor fire.
But if it had to perish twice,
I think I know enough of hate
To say that for destruction ice
Is also great
And would suffice.

'Fire and Ice' by Robert Frost

Contents

Prologue

Dear Annie,

I'm walking along the woodland tracks in Polkemmet Country Park, ten minutes from my house. It's so beautiful here – the sun streams through the trees and dapples the ground with bright beams of light, picking out the stones and rocks by the tinkling stream at my feet. Here, it is peaceful and quiet. I come here a lot – especially when the noise of the world gets too loud. I walk through the dense woodland, listen to the babbling of the river at my feet and suddenly I feel calm. And I think of you.

The fact is, you are never far from my thoughts. Every day, you are the first person I think of when I wake up and the last person in my mind as I drift off every night. You are the beating pulse of life. In my cupboard I keep the clothes you were wearing when you were just a wee baby. The pink and white babygros I dressed you in, the crocheted yellow cardigans that kept you warm. Everyone says I should get rid of them – but I can't. I suppose I never really learnt how to let go of you.

And yet, these words are all I have now. According to your adoptive parents' wishes, we are not allowed any physical contact, and though at the time I felt cheated, today I understand. You see, I've grown up a bit since we last met – when you were just two years old and I was fourteen. I've come a long way and though I know I've still got a whole mountain to climb, I feel it is time to tell you a little about me, my life and why we are apart. Because, Annie, my beautiful girl, I don't want you to ever think that I didn't want you. I did. Very, very much.

A lot was written about me back in those days. A lot of things were said that just weren't true. It's funny how people you've never even met can form an instant opinion about you just because they've read something in the paper. 'Twelve-year-old Mum!' – it made a good headline. It wasn't such a good life. But people didn't know the truth back then – they said horrible, hurtful things about me. Later, I realised that I had been used, taken like a lamb to the slaughter. But I'm not angry anymore and I suppose I don't care about those people. I have learnt to accept what happened to me in the past and move on with love in my heart.

Here is the truth: Annie, I always wanted you. And I loved you with all my heart. No, I didn't want to give you up and even though I was very young, I knew I could take care of you if they just gave me the chance. So I fought. I fought all the way to court and in the end the judge convinced me that I was not doing the best thing for you. He said I was being selfish.

And he was right – I couldn't give you the life you deserved. I wanted you to have a better life than I had – but I couldn't give you that. So instead, I gave you away to someone who could.

Annie, this is my story. And it is yours too. I hope that it helps you to understand what happened to us both and why. I hope that you can forgive me and perhaps, one day, we can be a part of each other's lives again. For now, I just want you to know that I love you – I always have and I always will.

You are forever in my heart.

Mum x

November 2014

CHAPTER 1

Going Away

The headlights of a car streaming through the thin curtains woke me early. For a moment I didn't know where I was. The yellow floral sheets on my bed were unfamiliar, as were the dresser, wardrobe and bedside table. My eyes scanned the room – it was a pretty, simple bedroom with cream curtains and a green carpet. How long had I been here? The only thing I recognised was my Monkey, tucked up safely under my arm – a well-worn brown teddy I'd had since I was a baby. After four years Monkey was beginning to look a little sorry for himself – he had bare patches along his body and pen marks all over his head where my wee sister had decided to give him some crazy body art with a felt tip. But I didn't care – Monkey smelled like home and right now that was exactly what I needed. I gave him a giant squeeze and sniffed in his comforting, familiar scent. I thought of Mum,

Dad and my big brother. Where were they now? I had no idea. I knew one thing only: today was Christmas Day.

As I lay there in the early hours, my mind wandered back to the day before. Mum, crying in the offices of social services.

'Can't you help us?' she sobbed. I had been looking after my wee sister Dionne, who was still just one year old, three years younger than me. Dionne loved it when I played Pat-a-cake with her and we'd been slapping each other's hands for a while now but as Mum started to cry, I ran to her and grabbed her round the waist. I hated to see my mum upset.

'I'm afraid it's the only option we can offer at this time,' the woman said. She seemed kind, in her brown flouncy skirt, ruffled white blouse and glasses which had slipped right down to the end of her nose. Her eyes were all wrinkled and I could see she felt sorry for my mum.

Mum was sniffing now and wiping her nose with a hanky, shaking her ponytail side to side.

'I can't go back to him,' she said quietly. 'Not after what he done to me. I'd rather be on the streets.'

'The children need a place to go,' the woman said gently.

There was a pause.

'Aye. Aye, I ken that.'

Silence again – then Mum looked from me to Dionne and that seemed to make her mind up.

'Aye, well, if there's nothing else, there's not really any choice, is there? I better get them packed up.'

I didn't really understand any of this at the time. All I knew was that we were going to get help from social services because Daddy had beaten my mum the night before. It wasn't the first time – it had been going on for ages, as far back as

I could remember – but this time he had really hurt her. Her terrified screams from the kitchen had made us jump up and run to her but the moment we got close, Dad turned to us all and snarled: 'Go upstairs!'

'But, Mummy!' I wailed, seeing my mum lying on the floor, one hand to her bleeding lip, and her hair and clothes dishevelled.

'I SAID GO!' Dad barked. My older brother Jason and I flinched, scared of what he might do if we didn't obey. We scampered up the stairs but we didn't go to our rooms. Instead we sat on the landing, both of us terrified of the smashing and screaming we heard from the kitchen. I was grateful my eight-year-old brother was there too – whenever I was scared, Jason was always there to comfort me.

The next day Mum's cheeks were all swollen and her eyes were puffy. Her voice sounded strange and low when she told us we had to leave Dad, for our own safety. It was only when the car came to collect us later that day that I realised what was really happening.

'You and your sister – you have to go and live with a nice family for a while. Just while I get everything sorted out,' Mum explained.

'Aren't you and Jason coming too?' I asked in a small voice.

'No – we can't.'

I started to cry then and grabbed my mum round the waist, determined that I would not let her go. If I didn't want to go then she couldn't make me!

'Hush now, Tressa,' Mum soothed. 'You've got to be a big brave girl and look after your wee sister Dionne. She needs you to be the grown-up one and show her there's nothing to be scared of.'

'But why can't you and Jason come too?' I wailed. 'I don't want to go away. I'm scared. I want to stay at home.'

'We can't,' Mum sighed. 'There isn't room. Your brother has to go somewhere different. But don't worry – we'll all be together again soon. I promise. We won't be apart long. Now stop your crying and be strong. Your sister needs you to be strong.'

My eyes filled with tears then, as I lay in bed recalling our difficult journey to the foster carer's. I felt lonely and terrified as the car drove away from my home in Broxburn, in West Lothian, leaving my mother and brother, stood on the pavement, watching us go.

Why were we being sent away? I just couldn't understand it.

Poor Dionne didn't have a clue what was going on and cried the whole way. I kept trying to put her dummy in her mouth but she kept spitting it out again to scream the place down. The social worker drove us half an hour through Edinburgh to get to a small house in a quiet street. The old lady with grey hair who greeted us in the doorway was smiling and sweet – I noticed the hallway was filled with sparkly Christmas decorations.

'Welcome, girls!' she beamed at our miserable, tear-streaked faces. The social worker lifted Dionne out of her car seat but she wouldn't stop crying until she was sat in the living room, next to me. She clung to me for dear life.

On Christmas Eve, a stranger called Janet put my little sister to bed while I sat in her living room with another foster girl, watching TV. It was weird and uncomfortable, and my mind couldn't focus on the programme. I just kept thinking:

This isn't right! I shouldn't be here! I should be in my own home with my brother and my mum. Janet's house was nice enough – she had comfy sofas and gave us tea of sausages and spaghetti hoops, and her windows twinkled with soft fairy lights – but I didn't want to be there a single minute.

I noticed that under the Christmas tree there were lots of brightly wrapped packages, and two gifts to the side. I read the labels with my head tilted to one side: one said Tressa and the other Dionne.

'Your mum left them with us,' said Janet when I asked why she had presents for us. 'She wanted you to open them on Christmas Day.'

I tried to be a good girl, but shortly after Janet put Dionne to sleep in the box room, she started crying.

'Ma sister's crying,' I told Janet. I thought maybe she couldn't hear her.

'I know, pet,' she replied. 'She'll settle down soon enough.'

But the wailing went on and on and on. The louder it got, the more upset it made me but Janet just ignored her. So I jumped up.

'I'm going to go to bed now,' I told her and raced up the stairs.

When I pushed open the door of the box room, poor Dionne was standing up in her cot, red in the face and holding out her bottle. I knew exactly what she needed – but this was an unfamiliar house.

'Shhhh, Dionne,' I told her quietly, hoping Janet couldn't hear me. I didn't want her to think I was being naughty.

'You be nice and quiet, and I'll fill up your bottle for you.'

The moment she heard my voice, Dionne's face softened

5

and relaxed. She nodded gratefully. I took the bottle from her and crept along the corridor to the bathroom. But the taps for the sink were too high for me and there was no stool for me to climb on, like we had at home.

I looked around – there was nothing else for it. I unscrewed the bottle and lifted up the toilet seat. Then I dipped the bottle into the water until it started filling up. When it was halfway full, I pulled it out again and screwed the lid back on.

Dionne's tiny chubby arms reached out through the bars of the cot when she saw me coming back in with her water.

'There you go,' I smiled, as she took the bottle and started greedily sucking on the water. She slowly toppled sideways in her pink babygro and I pulled the covers over her so she wouldn't get cold. Now content with her water, she barely noticed as I crept out of her room again.

I walked straight across the landing to the room I'd been shown to a few hours before and shut the door. I didn't waste any time – I threw off my jumper and jeans, and put on my Winnie the Pooh nightie, then switched off the lights and climbed into bed with Monkey. Under the covers and away from the eyes of the foster carer, I cried myself to sleep.

Now I watched the light fill the room as the morning broke on Christmas Day. I thought of the previous Christmas: Mum had made a lovely dinner of turkey with tatties and sweetcorn, and my aunties had come over with their families. It was great – just being around everybody made me happy. I sighed. I wondered if we would all be together again next Christmas.

I remembered my mum's words: 'Just be brave and strong.

We won't be apart long. I promise.' So I put on my brave face and went along the corridor to wake my sister up on Christmas Day.

It turned out to be quite a nice day after all – Janet made a delicious lunch and afterwards we opened the presents from mum. I got a new set of colouring pens and she bought Dionne a cuddly kitten that squeaked when you squeezed it. That made Dionne giggle.

'And now – another little surprise,' Janet announced, before showing me out to the backyard. There, leaning against the wall, was a shiny grey and silver bike, about my height.

I looked at her questioningly.

'Now, mind, it's not *new*,' she said. 'But it is *yours*, while you are here.'

'Mine?' I said, astonished. 'Really? Are you sure?'

'Aye, I'm sure. It used to be another little boy's, but he's not here now and somebody better be riding it or what's the point of letting it take up space in our garage?'

I laughed then and took hold of the handlebars. It was a lovely bike and I couldn't believe it was all mine to ride. I was so excited I took the bike out that very afternoon. Sadly, Janet forgot to mention that the brakes weren't working and I took a painful tumble down the hill. It didn't matter – having a bike was a wonderful thing.

At first I asked Janet every day if Mum was coming to collect us. But soon I realized that it was pointless. The answer was always the same: 'Not today, sweetheart. It might be a little while yet.'

Once a fortnight we were allowed supervised visits with my mum, and then we would cuddle her like mad and she'd tell

7

us that she was trying her hardest to get a house so we could all be together again. After she left, I always cried my eyes out. I loved seeing her but when she was gone, I felt empty and sad. It didn't feel right that we couldn't live together. As for Dionne, she had become so attached to me that I could barely leave the room without her going into a complete panic. As the weeks passed and she learned to walk, she started following me about all over the place, even to the toilet!

The weeks slid into months and gradually I stopped wondering what our new house would look like or when we'd all be a family once more. I just took everything day by day – Janet was kind and there were usually one or two other foster children to play with in the house so I wasn't lonely.

One day Janet announced it was a special day because it was my birthday and she was taking us all to McDonald's for a treat. I was very excited – we never got to go to McDonald's. We all went on the bus – Janet, Dionne, me and two of the other foster children – and after we got off in town, Janet herded us into a bright yellow and red restaurant. I broke into a wide grin the moment I smelled the delicious wafts of fried chips and burgers. This was a fantastic treat!

'What do you want?' Janet asked me when we got to the counter. There was so much choice I couldn't decide but eventually I settled on some chicken nuggets in a Happy Meal box and we went to sit at a round table in a corner while Janet fetched a high chair for Dionne. I tucked into my meal, loving the sweet spicy sauce for dipping and the thin crispy chips.

Ten minutes after we arrived, a lady appeared, leading a big boy towards our table. The boy also had a tray with a

Happy Meal and he slunk down into the seat opposite us. Janet greeted the lady and then started speaking to the boy. I just carried on eating, not paying much attention, until the boy looked at me and mumbled: 'Happy Birthday Tressa.'

Janet looked down at me and nudged me in the side.

'Well, Tressa, aren't you going to say hello?' she prompted.

'Who is it?' I whispered back.

'This is Jason,' she smiled.

'Who?'

'Your brother, silly!' she scolded fondly. 'Don't you recognise him?'

'Aye, oh right,' I muttered and looked at the boy again. I didn't recognise him at all. The brother I remembered from our house all that time ago was young – this was a much older lad. There was something else – there was something harder, tougher about Jason, like he was ready to fight all the time. I tried to recall the brother I'd known all that time ago – we used to call him 'Pies' because he was always a big lad. The memory brought a smile to my face and in that instant I caught Jason grinning shyly back at me. I saw the softness then in his eyes and it all came flooding back.

'Hello,' I said, embarrassed. I didn't know what else to say.

'Hi Tressa,' he said. There was another long silence.

Then he asked me: 'What did you get?'

'I got nuggets,' I showed him the tray – I had already eaten three.

'Aye, those are really nice,' he grinned. 'I got a burger but I like the nuggets too.'

A little while later, a clown appeared and made balloon animals for us – I kept stealing sneaky glances at my brother.

Jason seemed really happy. He looked at me and Dionne a lot and tried to talk to us about Janet's house. I wanted to ask him about where he was staying, too, but I felt shy. After all, he was like a stranger to me now.

One day, out of the blue, nearly a year after we were sent to live with Janet, we were told it was time to pack our things. We were moving back with our mum. I was so happy I wanted to jump up and down – but instead I raced to my room and started opening all the drawers and flinging my clothes on the bed.

Finally – I was going home!

CHAPTER 2

Mum

'What is this place?' I asked my mum, as she showed us into a small flat in Edinburgh.

'This is your new home,' she said. 'For now. Look, you take Dionne upstairs and put your things away. I'll have tea ready soon.'

It wasn't at all as I had imagined it. I thought we were going back to live in our old house but this was a whole new town. Mum seemed distracted and when I asked her about Jason, she just muttered something about Dad and then walked off.

It was my aunty Marilyn who welcomed me back with a big hug and a warm smile. She was lovely, my aunty, and I'd missed her like crazy while I was away. Over tea she explained that our granny (Mum and Marilyn's mum) was very poorly and Mum was tired from looking after her a lot. We would be staying in this new council flat for now, just while Mum tried to get us sorted.

Over the next few weeks, we only saw our mum fleetingly. She was always at Aunty Marilyn's house with Granny. When she was at home, she seemed upset and quiet. She didn't want to talk much; she just sat in front of the TV, drinking. Marilyn took care of us most of the time, and the small flat seemed sad and quiet. I was beginning to miss the warmth and cosiness of Janet's house, and in particular having other children around.

A few weeks later, Granny died. Mum was very upset about this and after the funeral, she spent every night in the living room with her sisters, Marilyn and Joanne, drinking and talking about old times. Eventually, she told us we had to leave the flat, as we couldn't afford to stay there anymore.

'Where are we going?' I asked.

'Och, I don't know,' Mum sighed.

'Are we going back to Janet's? Will you come too?'

'I don't know!' she exploded. And I didn't ask any more questions. It seemed as though she didn't have any answers for me anymore.

It turned out that the only place where the council could house us was in Blackburn Homeless Unit, in West Lothian. The unit was actually a pair of large towers in Blackburn with thirty floors each. All the flats in the towers were similar and ours was a one-bedroom flat on the second to top floor, with a kitchen, living room and bathroom. I hated it from the beginning. There was damp everywhere and the place smelt awful. We didn't even have a TV so there was nothing to do all day but sit on our beds, staring at the walls.

'This won't be for long,' Mum reassured us when we

arrived on our first day. 'We'll just stay here while I get back on my feet. Then we'll get your brother back and everything will be fine.'

But that night I watched Mum as she sat staring out of the window, a look of utter despair on her face. I wished there was something I could do to make it better for her. I did my best – taking care of Dionne and trying to help Mum whenever she needed it – but I couldn't take her sadness away. I couldn't magic up a new house where we could all live: me, Dionne, Mum and Jason. I wished I could. Jason was never far from Mum's mind – she talked about him all the time and whenever we were out, she would point out little boys who looked like him.

'I wonder what he's up to now,' she would say, staring into the distance, a dreamy look on her face. 'I wonder if he's missing us too.'

By now I was nearly six and I was proud that I could help my mum around the flat. It was a lot of hard work. There wasn't much money and we only had one set of clothes each so every night Mum had to go down to the electricity meter to put 50p in – enough to wash our clothes. There were lots of visits from social services and before each one, Mum got very anxious and nervous, running round the flat with the J-cloths and cleaning spray, trying to make everything look lovely and perfect. There was no TV, so often Dionne and I helped out with the cleaning and when Mum got fed up with us 'under her feet', she sent us into the bedroom to play.

One evening, Mum's mobile phone rang and she picked it up in the kitchen. I was doing some colouring in the lounge so I didn't pay Mum any mind at first – but then her voice got louder and louder.

'He's what?' she screamed. 'He's done what?'

There was a pause then, as Mum listened to the person at the other end of the phone.

'But he promised me!' she said. 'He promised me he'd look after him, that he'd take care of him until I got back on my feet. Why didn't he call me first? I could have done something…'

Mum's voice trailed off for a bit – she listened again, and I listened to her.

'But the boy needs his family. Why can't he come here?'

Silence.

'Of course I can cope! You know that – you've been here. I'm doing my best here and I'm proving it to you…'

Another pause.

'It's not right. It's just not right that Jason is put away in the YPC.'

I'd heard of the YPC; it was the Young Person's Centre – the place they sent kids when there was nobody who could or would foster them. Now I knew what Mum was upset about: somehow Jason had ended up in the YPC. I was confused because I thought he was living with our dad.

'No wonder he's angry!' Mum went on. 'He's not got his ma or pa with him. I just don't know why his father didn't call me first. I could have done something.'

Ten minutes later Mum came back into the lounge, this time with a can of White Lightning cider. She seemed agitated and shouted for me to put Dionne to bed. These days Mum got me to put Dionne to bed all the time. My little sister wouldn't settle down for Mum anymore. I guess it was because we'd never been separated and we'd spent a long time apart from our mum.

Poor Mum – I felt so sorry for her. None of this was her fault but it seemed that no matter how hard she tried, she couldn't make it work. At night I lay in bed worrying about my mum, hoping she would be okay. It was something I was used to. From the youngest age, I had worried about her – especially when Dad was angry with her or when he'd had a drink or two. Then his temper was frightening. There were a couple of times when the fights had got so bad that Mum had packed her bags and left Dad. It was on one of these occasions, when Mum had taken us to live with Granny, that something terrible had happened to her.

I was three years old at the time and the only other person who lived in the house with us was Granny's boyfriend Jon. We thought it was funny that Granny was so old and she had a boyfriend but he wasn't the type to laugh much. In fact, Jon usually kept himself to himself and sat in the living room with the paper or watching TV. At night I bedded down next to Mum's bed on a mattress on the floor, while Dionne, who was just a baby, slept in the cot. At the time Mum had a job as a chambermaid in a hotel, which meant that she had to get up at 6am to start work every day. Since she was up in the night with my wee sister too, it meant that she was always exhausted!

One night I was curled up fast asleep on the floor, when the sound of the door creaking open woke me up. I could only dimly make out the hunched figure of Jon silhouetted by the light on the landing and for a minute my head was fuzzy. I listened for the familiar sound of my mum's breathing on the bed just beside me and was comforted when I heard her soft, raspy snore. Mum had been given some pills by the doctor recently to help her sleep because she said she had had too many broken nights. I thought Jon was just checking on us and once he saw we were all okay, he would close the door and go away – but he didn't.

Instead, he padded softly towards Mum on the bed and leant over her. I couldn't see what he was doing then because it was above my head, so I sat up. I saw that Jon had pulled Mum's covers back and was lifting up her nightie with one hand. In the other he held a pair of scissors.

He caught me then – and I guess I must have looked confused and alarmed.

'Shhhh!' he whispered, putting his finger to his lips. 'Go back to sleep!'

I was a bit scared of him so I lay back down again, where I couldn't see him, but I didn't go back to sleep. I heard some funny noises and then, a few minutes later, he left. As soon as he was gone, I sat up again and went over to Mum – she was still snoozing like a baby. So I shook her:

'Mum! Wake up, Mum!'

'What? What is it?' Mum looked annoyed and very dopey.

'Mum – Jon was here. He did something to you. He told me to go to sleep but I didn't. I think he touched you. He had scissors.'

'What?' Mum looked horrified and furious at the same time. For a moment I wondered if she would believe me. She got out of bed and as she stood up, her knickers fell down around her ankles in two pieces.

'Oh my God!' She shook her head in dismay. 'The dirty, dirty bastard!'

She ran out of the room to fetch Marilyn. Marilyn stayed with Dionne in the house while she took me down to the police station, right then in the middle of the night. We gave our report to the police and they arrested Jon the next morning. It was a horrible thing but I was glad to have been there for her. I still didn't know what he did but I knew it was wrong. Poor Mum – all I wanted was to protect her and help her. She had gone to Granny's for safety and protection, and look what had happened! It sometimes felt like the world was against her!

Over and over she tried to prove herself to the social workers.

'We've got to make them see that everything here is okay,' Mum would tell me before another visit, as she scrubbed down the sink. 'Then they'll give us a house and we can get your brother back again. If they can see that it's all working out fine, we'll get the house.'

The social workers always came round with their fixed smiles and clipboards, asking us questions about how we were getting on. Mum tried her hardest but it was a strain on her and after each visit, she would collapse back on the sofa with a cigarette, exhausted.

We spent a lot of time in our flat in Blackburn – I was nearly ready to go to school but Mum said she didn't want me to start somewhere and have to move, so I stayed at home. We tried to ignore the shouts and the fighting noises that came through the thin walls at nights. And we were told we weren't allowed to speak to any of the strange men or women who hung around at the bottom of the stairs. Mum said this was a safe place because there were staff that lived on the block – still, she made sure she double-locked the flat door whenever we were inside.

Most days she would take us to the park across the road, and Dionne and I went on the swings and the slides. I made friends with one lassie who stayed across the corridor from us in the same block. Her name was Tara and because she was eleven years old, a big girl, Mum said I could go with her to the park on our own some days. That felt really grown-up. I liked playing with Tara because I didn't know many children.

One day Tara and I were playing on the monkey bars in the park when a group of big girls I'd not seen before came over to play. Tara immediately jumped down and went over to them – it seemed like they all knew each other. I wanted to go over too but I was scared. They were so much older than me. I thought Tara would call me over so we could talk to them together but she never did.

'Tara!' I called out.

'Aye – what d'ya want, Shrimp?' she shouted back over her shoulder. She never usually called me shrimp or spoke to me like that. I was surprised.

'Nothing – it's just, erm, it's getting on for tea time and...'

'Aye, and I suppose you've got to go back to yer mammy!' she teased. 'Does the little baby want her mammy? Eh?'

I felt the heat rise up in my cheeks, as all the other girls started to laugh at me. I was still clinging fiercely to the monkey bars.

'No!' I retorted angrily. 'I'm just saying, s'all...'

At that moment Tara came over to me and launched herself up on the monkey bars so that she hung facing opposite me; there was a new, mean glint in her eye.

'Do you want to go home, little girl?' she sang. 'Fine! I'll help you down!'

And at that she swung herself forward and wrapped her legs around my waist. She hooked them across my back then and started to pull me off the bars.

'What are you doing?' I yelled. She was so much stronger than me and her legs were so long; my arms soon ached and I didn't have any choice but to let go. I hit the ground awkwardly – humiliated now in front of the other girls who were laughing their heads off.

Tara jumped down and gave me a little shove: 'Go on then!' she sneered. 'Go on home to yer mammy! We don't want you here anyways.'

I didn't know why she was being so horrible but I didn't stay around a moment longer – I could feel the tears springing up behind my eyes and I wasn't going to let her see me cry. So I ran off, the girls' laughter still ringing in my ears.

That night Mum asked me what was wrong and why I was being so quiet but I didn't want to tell her. I still didn't understand why Tara had been so mean to me. Instead, the next day, I went to call on her as usual. I figured maybe she would tell me what was going on. But when I rang the doorbell and Tara answered, she looked even meaner than before – angry even.

'What are you doing here?' she yelled.

'I just thought...' I started, but she didn't give me time to finish.

'Just beat it!' she yelled and with that she gave me an almighty shove, so hard in fact that I nearly toppled backwards down the hard stone stairs behind me.

'And don't be ringing on this bell again!' she said, as I teetered uneasily on the top step. Then she slammed the door in my face. I was so shocked I didn't know how to react. I just didn't understand what had happened or why she had become so mean to me. I thought we were friends. It made me sad for a bit – after all, I didn't have any other friends. We didn't get many visitors either. Occasionally, our aunties would drop by and we loved seeing them, especially my aunties Joanne and Marilyn, who were both very kind and loving. But it was quite lonely in the homeless unit and I hoped that things would get better soon.

A few months later, Mum told us that we were moving to a new house.

'It's going to be a fresh start for all of us,' she said. 'Isn't that exciting? It's in Armadale – where your aunty Joanne lives. It's a nice place and it's got three bedrooms so we'll be able to get Jason back soon.'

I was so pleased and I gave my mum a big hug. I was tired of climbing the stairs to our flat every day. Up here, at the top of the tower, it was lonely and boring.

But still I couldn't help feeling a prickle of jealousy. *Jason! He was all Mum ever talked about. What about us?* I wanted to shout sometimes. *We're right here! Why don't you talk about us? Why doesn't your face light up when we're around the way you smile when you think about him!* Still, I couldn't be angry. I knew Mum had worked very hard to put our family back together again and now her dreams were going to come true. It was just what we needed – a fresh start! A new home! Now everything was going to be fine, just fine…

CHAPTER 3

Armadale

'How about that then?' Mum stood back from the wall to admire her efforts, a spray can in one hand, stencil in the other, and silver streaks smeared all down her jeans and across the bridge of her nose. I looked at the wall and smiled: 'Aye, that looks great!'

It was late September, just before my seventh birthday, when we finally moved into our new house at 23 Caulder Crescent. The house had three bedrooms and one of the bedrooms was just for Dionne and me.

When Mum had asked me how we wanted it decorated, I told her without hesitation: 'I want it to look like the stars at night!'

So the following day Mum took us to B&Q to buy some glow stars, spray cans and cardboard squares. We spent the rest of the day making stencils out of the cardboard and then Mum used them to spray-paint lovely silver stars all over our bedroom walls. She stuck the glow stars on the ceiling so that at night we would be able to see them in the dark. It looked fantastic.

'Aye, well it's your room so you better like it!' she grinned.

Armadale was the small town where we were all making our 'fresh start'. Mum told us that Dad was never coming back – not after what he did to her – so for now it would just be the three of us. Just for now, she added. It was so good to have a place of our own, finally. We had spent so many years moving about, so much time feeling uncertain and anxious about our future that I was relieved we would be able to stay in the same house all together. For the first time in a long while, I started to feel settled and happy.

Mum enrolled me in the local primary school in Armadale and asked the council if they could help out with money for the school uniform. When they refused her, she asked some of our new neighbours for help.

Luckily, there was a mum in our cul-de-sac whose daughter, Jenny, was in the same class as me and since she was a big girl, in all senses, she offered us Jenny's old school uniform.

'Aye, that looks nice and smart,' Mum said appreciatively when I got the clothes home to try on, the week before I was due to start school.

'But it's too big,' I protested, waving my arms around with the ends of the jumper flapping loose at the end. I looked down at the bottom of the trousers, which went straight to the floor and covered up my shoes. The waistband too was very baggy, which meant it felt like they were falling down the whole time.

'Never you mind about that!' Mum snapped. 'They'll do fine for now. Just roll up the sleeves at the ends and turn up the bottom of the trousers. They're meant to be big so you can grow into them!'

I felt a little silly on my first day of school – with my sleeves all rolled into a thick bunch at the ends and my huge turn-ups – but I didn't really have any choice. We couldn't afford a new uniform so this was what I had to wear. As we approached the old school building, my heart suddenly started to beat very fast.

'Do I really have to go, Mum?' I asked in a tremulous voice. I was almost seven, which meant I had to go into Year 3, where everyone knew each other already. I was scared they would be mean to me and nervous, too, that I wouldn't be able to keep up with the work – after all, I had missed nearly two years of schooling. Mum had done her best – she read to us every night and because I loved reading, she helped me learn to read and write. She would ask me to write little stories for her and I loved this so much.

'Och, you'll be fine,' Mum smiled, pushing me ahead of her, through the imposing school gates. It was a big place and reminded me of an old church. There were large rectangular windows and a turret right at the top. To one side, part of the building had been boarded up, and I imagined all sorts of monsters and ghosts probably lived inside that bit. Mum pushed me on again and in another second I was through the gates and into the playground, surrounded by other children and their mothers.

As it turned out, I really liked school. I made friends easily and found that there were a few who lived on my estate. Jenny and I quickly became close, and I enjoyed going to play at her house because she had a swingball set in her garden. There were a few others – Sophie, Anne and Susan. We all lived close by to each other, which meant that we could pop into each other's houses and Mum didn't mind.

The only trouble was that Dionne still followed me around like a lost puppy. And after I started school, it got much worse because she was away from me so much. Once I was back at home, she wouldn't let me out of her sight for a second.

'Och, Dionne, would you just leave me alone, please?' I begged one day after she had followed me from the living room to the bedroom, to the toilet and back again. The day before, I had tried to leave the house to play with my new friends but Dionne insisted on coming too and Mum said I should just take her.

'She gets in the way!' I protested to Mum.

'She's your sister – she hasn't got anyone else!' Mum replied.

'Aye, that's not my fault, though, is it? I just want some time with my friends.'

It was a complete nightmare – Jenny and I spent the whole time trying to play swingball but Dionne wouldn't stop walking between the string and pole, which meant that we couldn't hit the ball properly without fear of walloping her in the head. Finally, I'd had enough.

'Just leave me be!' I exploded. Dionne's bottom lip wobbled, then her face screwed up tight and a second later, she started to wail.

'I want Tressa!' she screamed.

'NO!' I yelled back.

She was crying so much she was hysterical. She threw herself on the floor and screamed and screamed and screamed. She was so upset that she turned red and she could hardly catch her breath. Her screams and sobs now mingled to produce a big gulping wheeze and a second later, she passed out.

'Oh Jeez!' I exclaimed as I bent down to check on my sister. Poor Dionne! I felt so sorry for her – she adored me but I wasn't her mum. And I just wanted friends of my own. It didn't take long before Dionne's little eyelids fluttered open and, seeing that she was okay, I decided now was the time to leg it.

'Mum, I'm going out!' I called as I headed for the door. 'I'm not taking Dionne today.'

'But can't you just…?' I could hear Mum coming through from the kitchen and I didn't stay to hear another word. I raced out the door and slammed it behind me. This was my new life, my fresh start, and I wanted to play with my friends on my own.

At first, it was just me, Mum and Dionne in the new house. Mum made a few friends in our area and at the weekends she was invited to go over to some of our neighbours' houses so Aunty Joanne came to mind us. We loved it when she came round.

'You go on out, have a good time!' Joanne told my mum. 'You deserve to enjoy yerself a wee bit.'

It's true – we all wanted Mum to enjoy herself. The only problem with Armadale was that people enjoyed themselves a lot around there! Mum was invited to parties every night of the week. She wasn't interested in going out all the time, though – she wanted to make sure to impress the social workers, so most of the time, she stayed in with us.

Occasionally, we'd see my dad – but now he was with

another woman and Mum said his drinking had got really bad. There were times he was meant to come and meet us but he never showed up. It was annoying but by this time I had got used to it and it felt normal. Anyway, I didn't want to see him when he was drunk because he could suddenly get angry for no reason. It was scary when he was like that.

Before long Jason started coming to visit at the weekends. He was very angry with my mum at first and he'd shout at her: 'You left me! You abandoned me!'

'It was nae my fault, son!' Mum pleaded with him. 'I didn't have any choice!'

'You took the girls!'

'I didn't! They were in care for a year. Your father promised me he'd take care of yous…'

On and on it went. Mum tried her best and after he left on Monday morning for the residential unit, Mum would apologise to us.

'He's just upset,' she'd say after he'd gone. 'Poor lad. Your father was meant to look after him when we split up. He promised me he wouldn't let them take him away. But then your dad did the dirty on all of us. He called the social services and had him taken one day, without even calling me first. That's how Jason ended up in the YPC – he just came home from school one day and the social services were waiting there for him. Your father betrayed him terribly. It's no wonder your brother's angry. I don't blame him for it.'

No, that was just the trouble – Mum never blamed Jason for anything! It seemed he could get away with murder while Dionne and I were always being told off for the tiniest little thing. Whenever Jason showed up, he was the golden boy who could do no wrong, even if he turned up with a policeman on his shoulder.

'He's been smashing windows again, Miss Tallons,' the policeman said the third time he brought Jason home in the van.

'What? My Jason?' Mum always seemed so shocked. She clutched at her chest in disbelief and shook her head. 'No way! Not Jason! Not my Jason. He'd never do anything like that!'

'Aye – he would and he did,' the policeman insisted in a tired voice. 'So now you keep him indoors because we don't want him causing any more trouble around here.'

Mum thanked the policeman and then put her arm around her 'golden boy', offering to fix him something to eat because he looked hungry. I always waited for the explosion – for the big TELLING OFF I was sure was coming his way. But it never happened. It almost felt like Mum was scared of him.

Later, I seethed silently as I watched Jason demolish bowl after bowl of cornflakes from a small box that was supposed to last me and my sister for the rest of the week. I loved my brother – after all, he was usually kind and good-natured with me. It was only Mum he shouted at. But I didn't understand why Mum didn't tell him off the way she told us off. I didn't understand at the time that she felt guilty. All I saw was that Mum only had one thing on her mind: getting Jason back for good. Week after week, she appealed to social services to let him come home. After all, we had the house now and there was plenty of room. If it was good enough for me and Dionne, then it was good enough for Jason too, she argued.

As hard as she tried, Mum struggled to make ends meet. As the winter drew in and the first frost arrived, our house got colder and darker. Mum's benefits never stretched far enough and by the end of the week there was never enough money left to put on the gas. Most mornings we woke up to see the clouds formed by our breath escaping from our mouths. If there was enough money for heating, it just went on the small radiator in the living room so we had one warm room and the rest of the house was freezing. Dionne and I would race out of the living room each night as quickly as we could to have a wash and brush our teeth in the bathroom before leaping into bed and snuggling under our covers. It was always a mad dash before our toes froze and our fingers started to prickle with numbness.

Mum bought enough food to last for a week but there were still times we didn't have anything for lunch.

'As long as you get one decent meal in you a day, it doesn't matter,' Mum told us when our stomachs ached from hunger. Mum was actually a good cook and she made the money last by cooking food that suited her budget – toad in the hole, spaghetti bolognese and pies. Even so, as she scraped together the last of her pennies, there were days when she realised that she didn't have enough to feed herself. So she would skip meals to ensure we had enough to eat. I hated those days – Mum was thin enough without denying herself food. And she had problems with her chest – asthma, she called it – which left her prone to colds. There were times I would catch her wheezing, and then she'd reach for the small brown inhaler she always kept in her pocket and take a few quick puffs. It always made me nervous when she wheezed. My mum wasn't tough; she was fragile and I did everything I could to look after her. I wanted to give her my food when we were short but she wouldn't hear of it.

'Don't be so stupid!' she scolded. 'You're a growing girl!'

During the week we were okay because we got free school lunches and then at weekends Aunty Joanne got paid from her cleaning jobs, so she would come over on a Saturday morning and bring brunch for us – usually ham salad rolls. My favourite. I loved it when Aunty Joanne came, especially as she always brought some toffees with her for 'afters'.

One Saturday in early December the doorbell rang and I jumped up from the sofa where I'd been watching TV, propelled by my empty, growling stomach.

'Aunty Joanne!' I screamed as I swung open the front door. But instead of my aunty standing on the doorstep, I saw Jason. He hadn't been home in ages and it was a surprise to see him. He looked older now and taller. He wore an earring, an Adidas top and a cheeky grin.

'Little sis!' exclaimed Jason. 'Just the wee 'un I wanted to see! How you doing, Squirt?'

And with that he enveloped me in a great big bear hug. It was lovely to see him! Mum wasn't far behind me and she shrieked when she saw that it was Jason at the door.

'Ma boy!' she said, taking him in her arms.

Aunty Joanne came along ten minutes later and we all sat round the table, munching our ham salad rolls, while Mum and Jason caught up. He was twelve years old now – a real big boy – and he seemed so much older than the last time I'd seen him. He was here for the weekend and then he had to go back to the YPC on Sunday night. I gathered from the conversation that Jason had been in a 'wee bit of bother' at the YPC but now he was trying to straighten out.

'So if it goes okay after a couple of months, they say they'll let me come back for good,' Jason concluded, picking the lettuce out of his roll.

'Oh, that is brilliant news. Isn't that brilliant news, Joanne?' Mum burbled excitedly. She couldn't take her eyes off him for a second – it was like she was hypnotised and kept touching him on the knee or the shoulder, just to check that he was real, that he was here.

'Aye – well I'm sick to death of that shithole!' Jason said bitterly. 'I don't want to be there any longer than I have to. It's a bloody madhouse!'

'You just got to keep yoursel' on track, love, keep your nose clean and don't get into any more trouble...' Mum instructed.

'Aye, don't worry about that,' Jason said, smiling winningly at her. 'I've stopped all that shite now. I just want to come home. This is a nice house.'

'And we just want you home, love,' Mum grinned at him, mussing up his hair affectionately. 'Isn't that right, girls?'

'Yeah!' Dionne and I chorused. I loved my brother and I wanted him home. We'd been separated too long and it felt like all the trouble and anger from before had left him. I understood he'd felt lonely on his own and I knew that he just wanted to be with us, his family. Most of all, I wanted him home so that Mum could finally be happy. It felt like everything was falling into place. The family was coming together and for the first time in years we were back on track...

CHAPTER 4

Jason

It was a cold Saturday night in December and Jason was back for the weekend. Now Jason – or Jay as we all called him – was here almost every weekend. Mum loved having her boy in the house again, especially because when Jason was around, he could babysit us while she went out. And Mum being happy – well, that meant everything to me.

'Are you lot going to be alright?' she yelled as she dashed about, picking up her keys, fags and lipstick, and stuffing them into her hoodie pockets.

'Aye, don't you worry none!' Jason called back as we sat watching TV together in the lounge. Dionne was already in bed asleep.

'I won't be late,' Mum said, planting a brief kiss on Jason's forehead, and then walked to the door. No kiss for me.

'Bye!' I called after her and seconds later I heard the front door slam. A minute later I heard the spark of a lighter and

Jason sucked in a deep lungful of the joint he had been keeping in his pocket. He always waited till Mum went out before lighting up. He told me not to say anything to her and I didn't because it was really none of my business.

We sat in silence for a few minutes as the clouds of fragrant smoke wafted around my head, and Jason inhaled again and again.

'Come and sit here!' he patted the empty cushion on the sofa next to him. So I got up off the floor and went and sat down. I was too caught up watching *Pop Idol* to notice, but a second later I looked down and saw that Jason had undone his jeans and had his *thing* out, which was all big. Now he was rubbing it with one hand as the joint hung loosely from the fingers of his other hand.

When he saw me looking, he nodded towards the TV.

'Just watch!' he instructed. So I did. I didn't know what he was doing and I suppose it didn't bother me so I just carried on watching TV. A couple of minutes later he got up and went to the bathroom.

That was how it started.

Two weeks later, Jason was babysitting again – this time he was upstairs in his room watching TV when he called me in. He was smoking a joint again and this time he said to come and watch with him on the bed. I did what he said and again he got his thing out. This time he told me to take my trousers off. I didn't understand why he wanted me to do this but I did what he told me. He inched himself over towards me and now he put his fingers *down there*.

'What are you doing?' I asked, confused.

'Never mind – just watch TV,' he said. So I did – and it

felt strange and uncomfortable but I didn't know what else to do so I just sat there while he touched me. He was my older brother so it didn't occur to me to say no to him. I just thought that maybe this was what all big brothers did. It didn't last long and when he stopped, I just got up, walked downstairs and went to watch TV in the lounge. It made me feel funny, what he was doing, but I didn't know why or what it was.

This carried on for a while – every time Mum was out of the house, Jason got his thing out and touched me in my private place. It wasn't nice but whenever I asked him to stop, he ignored me and often he'd blow the smoke from the joint in my direction, which would make my head go all funny. Then I didn't really know what was happening. All I knew was that I didn't like it.

Afterwards, I told him that I was going to tell Mum.

'You better not,' he growled.

'Why not?' I said, folding my arms.

'Because if you do, social services will find out and they'll blame her. Then we'll all get taken away and you won't see Mum ever again.'

I reeled at this thought – I couldn't bear the idea of being split up again, of never seeing my mum.

'But... but...' I started.

'Don't even think about it,' he said quietly, confidently, then took another big drag on his joint. He held his breath for a moment and then he slowly let the smoke out as a long thin line by pursing his lips together. I watched in silence. 'If you do, you'll split the family up, and then Mum will be on her own and she won't have any of us. Is that what you want?'

'No,' I whispered, shaking my head. It really wasn't what

I wanted. So I didn't tell Mum, even though I wanted to so much. I knew it wasn't normal anymore, what he was doing to me, because he said that if anybody found out we'd all get taken into care again. Which meant that what he was doing was wrong. Very, very wrong! But I couldn't tell anyone or Mum would lose us all. Now, every time she got ready to go out, I wanted to run and beg her not to leave me with Jason. He wasn't the kind, big brother I thought he was. He wasn't nice at all.

I didn't know what to do about Jason so I just tried to put it out of my mind. When I was at school, I tried not to think about it and then when I was home, I tried to keep busy so I didn't have time to remember the things he did to me. Nobody else knew and nobody could ever know – that's what Jason had said. If I told anyone, we would be put into care and it would destroy Mum completely.

Mum was now out a lot of the time and usually, when she had a drink in her, she was really happy. But there were times when she got really low and I didn't know how to help her. On my eighth birthday, I got home from school to find her crying her eyes out on the sofa. I had only seen my mum cry a couple of times before – when we got taken away and when Dad had hit her – so it was a shock. Not only that, she was crying so hard that it was like she couldn't breathe properly.

'Mum!' I rushed to her side. 'Mum, what's the matter? What's happened?' But she couldn't answer me, as she was crying too hard. She gasped, trying desperately to drag the air in to let her breathe and for a moment she looked like she might stop crying as she panted hard.

'Your inhaler!' I urged. 'Use your inhaler!'

She took out the inhaler, shook it and gave herself a couple of quick puffs. Then she broke down again. I didn't know what to do so I just sat next to her and rubbed her back.

Eventually, I got up to find Dionne, who was playing in our room, and I stayed up there with her for a bit. Mum carried on crying downstairs and my mind raced. *What was wrong with her? What if she couldn't stop crying? Would we have to be taken away again?* I was very nervous and upset, and couldn't concentrate on the card game I was supposed to be playing with Dionne.

After a little while, I heard Mum's voice calling my name, thick from the crying. I went downstairs and tentatively put my head round the door.

'Here,' she was holding out a hand full of change. 'Here – take this!' she insisted. I went over and took all the pound coins, fifty pence and twenty pence pieces from her.

'This is a tenner,' she said sadly. 'I've counted it out. It's a tenner. It's all we've got. Take Dionne to the shop and get yourself something nice for your birthday.'

I looked at her questioningly.

'Go on,' she insisted. 'Go and get a wee cake from the shop.'

Now my lips started to tremble. I was frightened. What was this all about?

'Mum – are you okay?'

'Aye, aye,' she said, wiping away fresh tears. Her face was all red and blotchy, and her eyelids so swollen I could hardly see her eyes. I started to cry too but I didn't know why. It was just awful to see Mum like this. I didn't care that it was my birthday. It made no difference to me, but Mum kept saying: 'Go on – take Dionne to the shop. I want you to go.'

So I went and got Dionne, put her shoes on and left the house, my pockets jangling from all the loose change. I was scared to go in case Mum wasn't there when we got back but I wanted to get the cake like she said. I suppose I wanted her to know she had got me something for my birthday.

We chose a Victoria sponge from the shop, paid for it with the change and walked home in silence. Fear now gripped the back of my throat and, with every step, I felt the panic swell in my chest. *Was Mum still there? What if she'd done something terrible to herself?* I opened the front door slowly, frightened to look inside. In the living room, Mum was still curled up on the sofa, sobbing. In some ways I was relieved – at least she was still here – but another part of me felt despondent. We needed help. We needed someone to help us. Mum couldn't cope on her own anymore. I had done everything I could but still she was utterly miserable. I wanted to say something to her then, to ask her to call Aunty Marilyn or Aunty Joanne. I wanted someone to come in and make things better. But as she had her back to us, it seemed that she didn't want to be disturbed.

'We got the cake, Mum,' I said quietly.

No response.

'I'll put the change down here.' I emptied my pockets onto the coffee table in front of her and the coins fell noisily onto the wood.

Still no movement and no sound. I took Dionne's hand and we went upstairs.

'What's wrong with Mummy?' Dionne asked innocently.

'I don't know, Dionne,' I said, biting my lip. We were both really upset and for a while we just sat there, staring at the cake, my birthday cake.

'Do you want to open it?' Dionne asked. I just shook my head.

'No, I don't want to either.'

Neither of us could touch it – I felt terrible for spending the last of Mum's money on a cake for myself.

The hours slid by and Mum didn't move off the sofa, not even to give us our tea, so reluctantly, Dionne and I ripped open the cake and we gobbled up the whole thing between the two of us. What else could we do? We were hungry.

As I put Dionne to bed that night, she gave me a really big hug around my neck with her tiny little arms. A hug so hard that I thought she was going to squeeze all the air out of me.

'Happy Birthday big sister!' she whispered into my ear.

'Thanks, Dionne,' I smiled sadly. It hadn't been a happy birthday at all. It was utterly, utterly miserable.

CHAPTER 5

Bernie and Pete

'Where is he?' I asked my social worker, June, for the fourteenth time that morning.

'I don't know!' she replied, in frustration. We were at the children's centre for our fortnightly contact visit with Dad. Dionne and I always waited excitedly for him to turn up but sometimes he just never showed. At first we'd been allowed to visit him in his home and they were always fun weekends. Dad would take us down to the river with his pals and their kids. The adults drank and us kids would play all day in the river, making dams, and catching fish and tadpoles. When Dad got too drunk to look after us, his girlfriend Maria would take over. I enjoyed it, especially as it was a chance to get away from Jason. But one time Dad got angry with Mum when she came to pick us up and he refused to hand us back. We found it scary and after that he was only allowed supervised visits at the centre.

I looked at the clock again – it was already an hour and a half past our arranged time. It made my blood boil. I was so excited every time and then, when he let me down, I felt so stupid and worthless for trusting that he would come. I knew what the problem was: Dad liked his drink too much. That was ALWAYS the problem.

'What should we do?' I asked June, who was now working on some forms. Dionne was on the floor with a colouring book and some pens – she didn't seem bothered about Dad. I wondered then if she'd just given up caring whether he came at all. June looked at her watch and then back up to the clock on the wall.

'We'll give it another ten minutes but after that we'll have to go, I'm afraid. I've got another conference in half an hour.'

He never came.

I tried to stay out of the house as much as I could now, since I didn't like to be left alone when Jason was there. He was living with us permanently and whenever we were in the house by ourselves, he tried to touch me and make me touch him too. I hated it so I just tried to avoid being there. Instead, I spent a lot of time with my friends Jenny and Anne. We were in and out of each other's houses all the time and they introduced me to one of the men who lived on our estate. Everyone called him 'Bernie' so I did too. Bernie had a second-hand car business and we used to help him polish up the old cars that came in so that they looked new and shiny again. Afterwards, he always gave us a few quid, which was great.

Mum never had enough to give us pocket money so it was nice to get something – just a pound here and there but to me it felt like being rich. Afterwards, I'd run to the sweet shop and buy loads of chocolates and sweeties, and gorge myself stupid!

Some days Bernie would give us a lift in his van to pick up spare parts or to look at old cars. I didn't tell my mum about going in the van because I knew she'd go mental if she found out, but we all thought it was fun and I liked getting the money for sweets. Back at his place he would give us all some Fanta and then hand out the money.

The first time something happened with Bernie, I was in his van on my own. He said he needed to collect an old car from a house. He drove us to a place I didn't recognise and then down a quiet street.

Once we got to the house, he looked down the driveway. There was no car in the drive.

'Ah well,' he sighed, peering out from the driver's seat. 'I guess they're not in. So we'll just have to wait.'

I sat next to him for a while, and then I saw his hand leave the gear stick and come snaking up towards my thighs. In another second his hand was on my leg and creeping upwards, towards my shorts.

'What are you doing, Bernie?' I said, swatting his hand away, but he was much bigger and stronger than me – a full-grown man – and my efforts proved useless. His hand was now down inside my shorts.

'Ach, come on, Tressa!' he said. In another second he had his fingers inside me and he was playing with his thing.

For a moment, I didn't know what to do. I was shocked but also frightened in case someone came out of the house and saw what he was doing to me. I tried not to make a sound and just prayed it would be over with quickly. It didn't take long. Afterwards, Bernie acted like nothing had happened but he gave me £4 when we got back that day.

'Just a little something extra,' he winked at me. 'For all your help today.'

I felt sick but I didn't object. I just took the money and ran out of there.

On other days we played in the old shed of a man who lived on the top floor flat of one of the houses in our street. It was a cool little greenhouse, and Anne liked to nick her mum's fags and take them there to smoke. We had asked him if it was okay and he said it was fine. He was really old and he liked to come down and watch us play.

'Just to make sure you're okay!' he'd tell us and then laugh to himself.

One day he came down and asked if we wanted to go up to his flat. Curious, we agreed and followed him up the stairs, though it was slow going, as he walked with a stick and swayed quite a bit.

'He's pissed,' I whispered to Anne behind his back.

'I know,' she squealed. 'Like a newt!'

His place was really small, and full of dusty old books and paintings. He lowered himself carefully down onto a grubby brown chair and then took a long swig from a glass of yellow bubbly liquid. He let out a satisfied sigh afterwards and then an unexpected burp. We all giggled at this and the old bloke looked at us then, as if realising we were there for the first time.

'What've you got there?' I asked him.

'It's cider,' he said. 'Do you want some?'

Jenny, Anne and I all looked at each other shocked and then started laughing. I was only eight years old and the other two were eleven and twelve!

'Are you serious?' said Jenny.

'Aye, why not? Just don't be telling your ma's,' he replied. 'By the way, I don't think I've introduced myself. It's Peter, well, Pete. Who are you girls?'

We all told him our names and Pete got us each a small glass and filled them up from a bottle of White Lightning cider. The sweet, bubbly liquid went straight to my head and I immediately started to giggle like crazy. By the time we left we were all falling about and even tumbled down a few of the steps of the block of flats.

'Mind how you go now, girls!' Pete shouted out after us. We thought this was hilarious.

So after that we all went round to Pete's a couple of times a week and whenever he offered us cider, we took it. He also gave us little bits of pocket money, which was great. Only it wasn't long before Pete started up too. I was on my own there one day, waiting for Jenny, when he came over to me and started to unbutton my shorts. I tried to tell him to stop but he wouldn't.

'Tressa,' he said. 'Just let me will ya? Just a little bit for all that pocket money I gi' ya.' And I didn't want to but I stopped struggling. I felt like I didn't have any choice. It almost felt like this was what was expected of me now. From Jason, from Bernie and from Pete.

I found myself very confused and lonely most of the time. I didn't tell anyone what was happening to me and I suppose I started to accept this was just part of my life now. The worst thing was the stuff with Jason – I felt very mixed-up about him. On the one hand, he was my big brother and I loved him. I looked up to him. But on the other hand, he made me do stuff that I didn't like. He never talked to me about it or mentioned it at all – in fact, around everyone else he acted as though everything was normal. So I tried to carry on as normal – I tried to put it out of my head.

But now that this was happening with Bernie and Pete too, I found I couldn't stop it coming into my head when I least expected it. And that made me feel dirty, ashamed and worthless. At school I tried to concentrate but I couldn't focus on the lessons. The only subject I really enjoyed was art and I loved drawing the best. But the rest of the time I found it a struggle. I felt like I was holding this horrible, dirty little secret inside me which made me different from everyone else. In bed at night, I asked myself over and over: why? Why were they doing this? I didn't understand it at all. And the confusion and frustration grew and grew.

I had so much anger inside me that I couldn't control myself. When the teachers asked me to settle down or told me off, I'd scream and shout at them, and sometimes I even ran out of the classroom.

Time after time I was sent to see the headmistress and there, in her office, all my anger spent, I'd apologise over and over for my bad behaviour. I didn't know what happened to me during these episodes – it was like I wasn't even there. I'd see red and then I'd feel this powerful surge just take over my whole body – and then I'd go blank. I'd come round half an hour later, feeling really dazed, not having a clue what I'd done. Then they'd tell me I was hitting, punching, kicking – really bad stuff. Mum was called in to school a few times but it didn't seem to help. The anger only got worse and worse.

'I don't know what's gotten into you, Tressa, I really don't,' the headmistress, Miss Caplan, said, tutting and scratching her head. 'I'm baffled. Why are you here AGAIN?'

'I don't know, Miss,' I replied, genuinely upset and sorry. I honestly didn't have a clue what I had done this time.

'I'll tell you why. It's because you picked up a chair today and threw it at Mrs Beckley,' she said. She paused then and looked at me intently.

'*Threw* it at her! Do you have any idea how much damage you could have caused? You were very lucky she didn't get seriously hurt, otherwise you would be looking at a permanent exclusion. We're very disappointed in you, Tressa.'

'Yes, Miss.'

'Very disappointed.'

I couldn't bear it anymore – I started bunking off school because that seemed easier. I ended up hanging around the shop up the road from us where there were loads of other kids, usually a lot older than me. Whenever I could, I used to help out Bernie and Pete so I could get money to buy fags and booze. And if they tried to touch me, well I just had to let them, didn't I? It was the only way I could get my money.

Sometimes I went up to Pete's and I drank loads of his cider so that I wouldn't notice so much what he was doing.

So this was Armadale. It was meant to be our fresh start. It was meant to make everything better. But in little over a year after moving here, everything had got completely out of control and my life was in pieces. The worst thing was, I didn't know how to make it stop.

CHAPTER 6

Losing My Way

A couple of months later, Jason came home on a Friday for the weekend and Mum took Dionne to the doctor's. I was in the living room watching TV and Jason was in the kitchen. After a few minutes he sauntered through and sat on the sofa. I could tell by the tension in the room that something was going to happen – I could just feel it. I sensed Jason's eyes boring into the back of my neck as I sat cross-legged on the floor in front of him.

'Tressa,' he said, very quietly. I didn't react.

'Hey, Tressa!' he said again, louder this time. I knew I couldn't ignore him forever.

'Yeah, what?' I was annoyed and a little frightened. I knew he had something in mind.

'Go through to my room and lay down on the bed.'

'No!'

'Yes. Do it!' he said. He didn't have to shout – I was only sitting right there – but there was something cool, cocky almost, about the way he spoke, like he knew I didn't have a choice.

'I don't want to,' I sulked, turning back to the TV. 'I hate it.'

'Do it now,' he said again. And this time his voice was so low and threatening that I knew I didn't have any choice. By now Jason had convinced me that if I refused anything then he would tell Mum himself what was happening and we'd all get taken off her. He made it seem like it was all my fault and I was to blame.

I got up slowly, reluctantly, and walked up the stairs then I threw myself onto Jason's bed and plunged my face into the pillows. A few minutes later, Jason came in with a joint in his hands. He took off his T-shirt then pulled down his jeans and his boxers. I didn't want to look so I just stuffed the pillow into my face. Then he climbed on the bed and pulled my jeans and my knickers off me. I lay there, frozen, not wanting to move or make a sound, frightened of what he would do next.

'Get on your knees,' he ordered. So I did. I was on all fours when he started to touch me – oh God, I hated it! It was horrible, horrible. This wasn't normal! This wasn't what normal brothers did; I knew that for sure.

Suddenly, a sharp pain shot up me, as his body pushed against mine. I gasped from the intense burning pain inside and then in another second he was pushing himself into me over and over again, making me shudder with agony. I just held tightly to the pillow and buried my head into it, trying to block out what Jason was doing to me. I screwed up my face and opened my mouth wide, in a silent scream. I felt awful and in such pain that I couldn't help crying. But still he kept thrusting against me and it felt like he was splitting me in two.

Finally, after what felt like forever, he pushed one last time very hard inside me and then let out a grunt. Then he pulled away and clambered off the bed. I lowered my body to the bed and stayed that way, not looking at him, not doing anything. I felt awful, sick and ashamed.

I listened to the sound of Jason doing up his zip and putting on the rest of his clothes. Then, when I felt sure he had left the room, I managed to push myself up to a sitting position.

Owww! It hurt like hell down there, and I had to move very slowly and carefully so I wouldn't give myself more pain. It was like he had ripped me in two.

Somehow, I managed to pull my knickers and jeans back on and then I limped to the bathroom across the hallway. I tried to wash myself down there with my hands but it was so sore it hurt and so I gave up. Instead, I splashed water over my face and leaned against the sink, panting against the pain.

'Hey – Tressa!' Jason's voice called out from downstairs. *Oh Christ – what now?* I didn't want to respond. I didn't want to see him again.

'Come down here!' he called. And so, with a very heavy heart, I opened the bathroom door and went downstairs.

Jason was sitting in front of the TV with another joint in his hand. He held it out to me then.

'Here,' he said, squinting against the swirling smoke around his head. 'Here, take this.'

I took it – I didn't know what else to do. Then I put the end to my lips and took a small tentative drag. The harsh smoke hit the back of my throat and immediately made me cough but this only made Jason laugh.

'There you go, little sis!' he smiled. 'Have yerself a wee smoke now.'

And I took another drag, but this only burned my lungs more and I passed it back to him, without a word. My head began to swim and I felt very strange.

'Don't yer want any more?' he asked, like he really cared what I wanted! I just shook my head and walked out. I went up to my bedroom, lay down on my bed and wept silently into my pillow.

For hours and hours and hours.

I was nine now and my head was a mess. The only thing that seemed to make all the horrible stuff in there disappear was drinking. When I was drunk, I felt so strong, so confident, like nobody could make me do anything I didn't want to. It made me feel invincible. So I bunked off school more and more to get drunk.

A couple of weeks later, I was hanging round the shop with Jenny when we saw a girl we knew coming out with three bottles of Lambrini. Her name was Sandra and she was a lot older than us but it didn't matter. I always seemed older to everyone around me. I acted older than nine, I looked older than nine and I felt a lot older too. We got chatting and she asked us if we wanted to go back to her place for a wee drink.

'Aye, why not?' I replied cheerfully. Jenny agreed to come too, though she never drank or smoked. She was a goody two-shoes. As soon as I tasted the Lambrini, I loved it! It was so sweet and bubbly.

For the rest of the afternoon Sandra and I necked all three bottles until it got dark and, finally, Jenny pulled me to my feet.

'Come on,' she urged. 'It's time to get back. It's really late.'

'So what?' I slurred. 'I don't want to go home.'

'Aye, you do!' she insisted and pushed me out of the door. I swerved and staggered all the way back to my house, giggling every time I fell over on the road or plummeted sideways into a hedge.

'Jesus!' Jenny exclaimed the third time she yanked me out of a bush. 'You're absolutely steaming!'

'I know!' I snorted back. 'I love it!'

I fell in my front door and Jenny raced back to her house. Mum was sitting on the sofa in the living room watching TV and when she saw me, she jumped up, furious.

'Where have you been all day?' she exploded. 'The school called – you never went in. I didn't know where you were. It's 9pm. Do you know that? I had to call the police.'

I was trying to get up the stairs so I could go to my room and sleep but as I moved across the living room, the floor seemed to disappear underneath me and I fell again.

'You're pissed out your head!' she said. 'Look at you! You can't even walk straight. Christ! I'll have to call the police back. They're out there right now, looking for you!'

'No you're fucking not!' I shouted back. What did she want to go and call the police for? It was stupid!

'Aye, I will. Just watch me!'

'What do you want to do that for, you fucking bitch!' I screamed.

'Don't you talk to me like that! Don't you dare talk to me like that. I'm your bloody mother and you have been missing!'

My head swam, my vision blurred and all of a sudden I felt a heaving sensation in the pit of my stomach. In another second a wave of nausea hit me and I threw up – right there in the living room.

'Ah, for heaven's sake!' Mum rushed to my side now and held my hair back from my face as I heaved over and over again.

I'd never been so drunk in my life before. Just a minute ago, I'd felt so happy and confident – now I was a wreck. I felt utterly wretched and miserable. I started to cry.

Mum mopped up my sick while I sat on the sofa and wept.

'You're grounded for a year,' she seethed as she mopped. 'And if you keep this up, you'll end up being put into care. Where have you been anyway?'

'I've been out,' I groaned, sore and sick all over. It felt like someone was hammering my head from the inside.

'I'm going to have to call the police back,' she muttered to herself.

I just stared at her – I couldn't believe she'd done that. Mum was not a fan of the police and she was always afraid of them turning up in case it meant social services getting involved.

'Oh aye,' she said. 'I called the police. What else was I supposed to do? A nine-year-old who disappears and doesn't come home. Eh?'

I let this sink in. The fact that she'd called the police showed she cared. She was worried about me, regardless of what it meant for our future.

By 10.30pm I was lying on my bed, ill and miserable, when the doorbell went. A few minutes later I heard heavy footsteps on the stairs and soon after that, two large policemen marched into my room.

'Tressa,' one of them started. 'Tressa, do you know what kind of trouble you've caused tonight?'

I didn't answer.

'Tressa, you've had your mother in bits and wasted a lot of police time with your disappearance today. Do you think that was the right way to behave? Not to mention underage drinking!'

Again, I didn't reply. What did they want me to say?

'We could take you down the police station right now and lock you in a cell to sober you up,' he went on.

Finally, I flipped out. I bolted upright and fixed these two men with my meanest stare.

'Go on then!' I yelled at them both. 'Go on and take me to the station! You're not going to put a kid in the cell and actually lock the door, and you know it. You're just trying to scare me!'

I wasn't stupid – I knew they didn't put kids my age in a cell with the door locked. I'd heard about it from my pal.

'Why don't you just get the hell aways from me!' I said, a bit calmer now but still woozy and sick from the Lambrini.

'This one has some cheek!' the first policeman said to the other one, thumbing in my direction. 'Aye,' the second one said. Then he turned to me: 'You're awful lippy for your age, young lady. You know you're going to get a fright one of these days.'

'Just fuck off and leave me alone!' I groaned. Then I put my head under the covers and turned away. Gradually, I heard them leave and the cop car drive off. *Stupid policemen*, I thought as tiredness now took over. *Stupid, bloody, interfering, lying, stupid…*

'SCHOOL TIME. GET UP! GET UP!' Mum's voice pierced my dreams and I awoke violently to a feeling that I was actually going to die. My head pounded, my heart hammered in my chest and the rest of my body was numb and unresponsive, as if in shock.

I may never be able to get out of bed ever again, I told myself. It didn't seem possible to feel this rotten. I'd drunk probably a bottle of Lambrini the day before, maybe more, and now I felt like I had been hit by a train.

Mum wasn't giving up. 'Get up Tressa! Now!' she yelled from behind the door.

'I can't!' I called back, immediately regretting trying to speak. My own voice reverberated inside my head, sending powerful and painful shockwaves to my brain that only compounded my agony.

'You can and you will!' she said firmly. 'You've bunked off too much recently. You're going in to school today and that's that.'

Somehow I managed to get myself up and dressed that day, and I dragged my wrecked body into class. I felt like I was going to be sick all day long and when I got home, I just collapsed onto the sofa. It was the worst hangover I'd ever had but it wasn't to be my last.

Two weeks later, Jason arrived on a Friday for the weekend. I was upstairs in my room and he stayed downstairs for a bit, chatting to my mum and Dionne. Half an hour later he came upstairs and into my room. He was wearing baggy jeans and his head was shaved at the sides. He cracked a smile – a genuine smile – and for a moment, for a millisecond, I imagined that he wasn't going to do something horrible to me that day.

Relief swept over me and I smiled back. Then he shut the door behind him and said: 'Lay down on your back, Tressa.'

My heart sank and I felt like crying. I wasn't allowed to refuse him – I knew that. I had to do whatever he said to stop them taking us all into care. I had to let him do what he wanted to protect my family.

He got undressed and took my shorts off but only to my ankles – he left my shoes on. Then he put his fingers into me and he kept pulling them out and shoving them back in again. In and out – it really hurt because his fingernails were sharp and they cut into my insides. I wanted to cry out with pain but I was afraid to make a sound in case someone heard.

Then he got on top of me and started to have sex with me. A few times it came out and then he wouldn't notice that it wasn't inside me, just sliding between my legs. I kept trying to do that so that he wouldn't hurt me and this time when he came, it wasn't actually inside me at all. A secret little note of triumph sounded in my head.

But just as he was pushing himself off me, I heard the handle turn in the door. Jason jumped away, hastily pulling up his jeans, which had been round his ankles. The next second Jason's mate, Alex, was in the room, looking as if he couldn't quite believe what he'd seen. Jason was still desperately hoisting his jeans to his waist and fumbling with his flies. I curled myself into a ball on the bed – but I was still naked. Alex was always round our place for Jason but this one time, I wished he would just turn around and leave. I was terrified. *Did he see? What if he told someone? Would we all end up being sent into care again?*

'What are yous doing?' Alex said, his eyebrows furrowed in confusion.

'Nothin',' Jason said hurriedly. 'Nothin', bro. Just teaching the wee 'un here about sex education.'

'What?' Alex looked really confused now and shocked. I was mortified. I couldn't think what else to do so I hid myself under the covers. This was agony – so humiliating.

'Oh forget about it!' Jason said, pulling on his T-shirt and taking Alex by the arm. 'Come on – let's get out of here.'

And with that, Jason hauled Alex out of the room. Once they'd gone, I scampered round, picking up my clothes and pulling them back on again. *Alex had seen! What would happen now?*

A wave of shame passed over me then, as I recalled the moment Alex had burst in on us. His shock had been so painful. And to think I had just lain there like a rag doll, not fighting him off or trying to stop him. This was the thing that embarrassed me the most. I felt like I had just given in to Jason completely.

After Alex had caught us, I kept waiting for something to happen – but it never did. In fact, the next time he saw me it was as if he'd never caught us in the first place. I guessed Jason had talked to him, told him he hadn't seen anything to worry about and Alex had just forgotten about it. During that time I was getting drunk a lot with my friend Susan and Pete at Pete's place. I liked the feeling it gave me and I didn't want to go to school anymore. By now Pete did what he liked with me and sometimes I was so drunk I didn't notice. Afterwards he always gave me a couple of quid for it. It made me angry. I'd heard about prostitutes and the way they had sex for money, and this is what Pete made me feel like

– a prostitute at nine years old! Still, I took the money and I bought booze and fags.

Mum had made her own friends in the area now and she was drinking a lot too. The partying would start on a Thursday night and go on till Sunday or maybe Monday. I could get away with more than ever before because once she was drunk, she didn't care so much; she also seemed a lot happier in herself when she had a drink in her. If she was drinking at her pal's house, either my aunty Joanne would come to look after us or Jason would be left in charge, which always meant one thing: he'd make me have sex with him.

On Christmas Day that year Mum locked herself away in her room all day with her new boyfriend, drinking. Then I started to hear this moaning and crying coming from her room. I sat outside her door, begging her to let me in. I thought he was hitting her, just like Dad did! But she kept telling me to go away. I sat there all day, terrified for my mum, and eventually I got so upset that I launched my foot straight at the door, kicking it open.

There, on the bed in front of me, were my mum and her boyfriend Adam, both completely naked. There was a long pause as we all looked at each other – I realised in that moment that Mum hadn't been crying in pain. She'd been having sex!

'What the fuck do you think you're doing?' Mum exploded, pulling the cover round her breasts.

I was speechless for a moment – suddenly, all my fear and worry for her turned into rage. We'd spent all of Christmas Day alone so she could have sex?

'What about the rest of us?' I yelled at her. 'What about the rest of your kids? Have you forgot about us or something?'

I was so mad at her. It was like she had given up trying to be a mum and now she was just ignoring us. Why didn't she care enough to even be around us on Christmas Day?

'You!' I pointed at Adam. 'Get out! Go on – get out!'

Mum said quietly: 'This is ma house, not yours. And I say he's staying.'

I could have punched her right then but instead I stormed out – all that time I'd been worried about her! She wasn't worth it.

One morning in January Mum told me to get ready because we were going to a children's hearing. I knew what one of those was – Mum had gone to a lot of them for Jason when he was in care. But I didn't know why I had to go this time. I wasn't nervous at all – in fact, I was a bit hungover so I was feeling ropey and tired when she took me along to Bathgate. There we were shown into a bare office with a big round table in the middle and five people sitting round it. There were June and Helen, the social workers, and two other panel members, plus a man who introduced himself as the chairman.

One by one, they went through all the different reports: health, social, school and police. They all said the same thing – I wasn't doing well in school; I was bunking off and getting drunk. On and on it went – they read out the police reports from all the times I hadn't come home and Mum had reported me missing. It was so dull. All I wanted to do was go back to bed and sleep for the rest of the day. I rested my head on the table and closed my eyes. It felt like I was drifting off while somewhere up above my head I heard the man's voice droning on…

'Miss Tallons,' the chairman said to my mum. 'We feel that Tressa is getting out of control and you are simply not coping. There are some very disturbing reports from the school – reports of violent outbursts and many examples of truancy – as well as police reports. Tressa has been noted to be both drunk and under the influence of drugs at times. At nine years old this is unacceptable. It appears that Tressa is without parental control.'

'No!' Mum said. 'No, she's not. I can change – really! I can do better.'

'I'm afraid we don't think it would be in Tressa's best interests to live at home right now. We feel Tressa would benefit from some time in a stable and disciplined environment where she can get the appropriate level of care.'

'What?' I exploded. Suddenly, I was wide awake. 'Are you putting me back into care?'

'We think it's for the best, Tressa,' the man went on. 'You can go back to your house to get your things and then Miss Drake here will collect you in half an hour.'

And that was it – I didn't have a choice. My fresh start was over and in that short meeting it was decided I was to be taken away from my family all over again. All that time I'd protected Jason, when I hadn't told anyone what was happening, had been for nothing.

CHAPTER 7

In Care

I cried all the way home that day – I didn't want to leave my mum and I especially didn't want to leave Dionne. We'd never been separated before. I was furious – why hadn't Mum fought harder for me? She didn't even seem that upset.

'This is all *your* fault!' I sniffed as I flung clothes into a small blue holdall.

'No – don't take that!' Mum fished out the jeans and T-shirts I'd put in just a second before.

'Why not?' I said.

'Because they'll buy you new clothes at the foster carer's place. Don't bother taking this other stuff. Just pack your nightclothes and your school uniform.'

Dionne sat on the bed, looking at me, fat tears plopping down into her lap. She didn't bother wiping them away. She just let them fall. I sat down next to her and put my arms around her.

'You'll be alright, Dionne,' I whispered into her ear. 'Don't worry. I won't be gone long.'

The truth was I didn't know how long I would be in care for but I hated to see my wee sister upset. How could Mum let this happen? After all I'd done to protect this family, after all the pain and shite I'd had to put up with from Jason, and now I was being taken away anyway!

It just wasn't fair.

The social worker was in the house in no time. The moment she arrived, I suddenly felt terrified. *Where was I going? Where would they put me?* Everything that I'd ever known was being ripped away from me and there was nothing I could do about it.

'I hate you!' I spat at my mother as I left the house, the small blue holdall over my shoulder.

'Aye, I love you too sweetheart!' Mum replied. She always did that and it annoyed me so much.

I got in the car with June, my social worker, and as she drove me away from my family home, she explained where we were going.

'Her name is Barbara Foxton,' she said. 'She's an older lady, very nice, very experienced. She usually fosters older children but she's made an exception in your case. There will be a couple of others staying there for now and you should be very comfortable. It's a nice house and a good family. Don't worry – you'll be well looked after.'

It turned out that Barbara lived in a really nice, big clean house with a lovely kitchen where the other girls – all teenagers – and I could hang out. Barbara herself was a soft, older-looking lady – probably around sixty – who wore her long grey hair in a bun and long skirts that touched the ground.

But from the word go, she was really strict about the rules.

'No smoking whatsoever!' she said firmly after she'd shown me to my room.

'If I catch you smoking – or if I even find any baccy in your belongings – then you're grounded.'

'Are you kidding?' I said. I couldn't last a day without a smoke!

'I'm not kidding,' she said. 'Not at all. You're nine years old. There's no way a child of your age should be smoking. And you're to come straight home after school every day – no hanging about the shop. Bedtime is 8pm sharp.'

'What?' I was outraged. I loved to watch all the soaps when I was at home and some of them didn't even start until 8pm.

That first night I got grounded when Barbara found baccy in my bag.

Now my life was miserable. I hated it at Barbara's. I wasn't allowed to go out, I wasn't allowed to smoke, and I had to be in school every day and in bed every night by 8pm. It was boring as hell and I missed my little sister. At the weekends I had nothing to do but sit in the kitchen all day watching TV. Then, Barbara would hand us a couple of quid and tell us to get our tea from the chippy opposite and we'd all have pie and chips. I was bored and lonely. At home I was used to looking after my little sister – there was always company for me and even if Mum was out, my aunties would come round. I missed my aunty Joanne's Saturday morning brunches. I missed the easy, comfortable way I could talk to my family. Living with strangers wasn't easy.

On top of all of this, I was dying for a smoke. All the other girls in the house broke Barbara's rules by smoking out of the bathroom window. I thought I'd try it myself but I did it in my bedroom instead, standing on my bed one morning as I lit up out the window.

Just my luck – Barbara's husband was on his way home from a night shift and caught me! I knew he'd seen me but I hoped he might let me get away with it just this once. No chance!

When I got downstairs half an hour later, dressed and ready for school, Barbara was waiting for me, mad as hell.

'What did I tell you about smoking?' she scolded.

'No smoking at all,' I mumbled. 'But I was desperate, Barbara!' I appealed to her to let me off but she wasn't having any of it. She took the rest of my baccy and my lighter from me, and made me turn out all my pockets.

'That's it,' she said. 'You were warned about the smoking and today I'm keeping you off school for breaking my rule.'

'You can't do that!' I objected

'Who cannae!' she bellowed. 'Now get up to your room! You're grounded!'

That day I sat in my bedroom, raging. The only place I got to go these days was school and now I was even being denied that! Admittedly, it had got a whole lot better recently. The headmistress had called me in to see her two days after my move to Barbara's.

'I'm going to make a deal with you,' she said in a level voice. 'I know that you like visiting the nursery so I have a proposition. If you behave yourself, stay in school, keep your temper under control and generally make an effort in your classes then I will allow you to spend every afternoon in the nursery. What do you think? Is that fair?'

I agreed to the deal immediately. It was true – I loved being in the nursery with all the wee 'uns. Most of the children were lovely and there was one girl in particular that I liked – her name was Annie.

On the first day of my new 'deal' I'd been appointed Annie's 'buddy'. She was four years old and from the word go, I thought she was just perfect. She was so sweet and quiet, and she had such beautiful, long blonde hair that made her look like a little angel. Every day, after lunch, I'd race into the nursery to play with her. We'd do finger-painting, play in the sand and plant things in the garden together.

There was something about her easy smile and her innocent nature that reminded me of myself many years before. Annie was quiet around the other children, and the staff told me that before I turned up she was bullied. But when I was there, she came out of her shell and her confidence grew.

I loved Annie so much – playing with her allowed me to be a child again. I could sit for hours with her in the sandpit just sieving sand from one bucket to the next, building castles or drawing faces with the tips of our fingers. For a short while, I could forget about all the stuff back home – about all the problems with Jason and Mum, Pete and Bernie – and lose myself in a simple, joyful game. Down there, in the sand, focused on the tiny grains, my world shrank to miniscule proportions and nothing else seemed to matter apart from what I was doing that very second. It all fell away and, for a while, it was just me and Annie, playing side by side, completely absorbed by the sand and the patterns we could make with our hands. This was our world and we were in control.

In the nursery, nobody judged me or wanted anything from me. They were kids – they didn't care if I was running about shouting and having fun. It was the only place I felt I could relax and truly be myself. For the first time in ages, I was happy in school because it gave me access to a world I felt I had lost a long time before.

Sitting in my bedroom at Barbara's, I was annoyed at missing a day at the nursery, a day with Annie. And of course I was dying for a smoke. Even though I knew I wasn't meant to, I usually managed to grab a smoke most days by running all the way back to my mum's home from school each lunch time. She'd give me a fag, we'd have a quick chat while I smoked it and then I'd have to run all the way back to school again to get back in time for the afternoon bell. It meant I could see her briefly, get my nicotine hit and make sure that everything was okay.

After six months, during which time I turned ten, I was told by the social workers that I was going home. My behaviour and school attendance had improved, and it turned out that Barbara was now retiring and selling her big house so she couldn't look after any of us anymore. By now, I had got used to living with her and I felt a little sad at leaving.

'They couldn't find another foster replacement,' she explained the night before I left, as she stood in the kitchen, ironing sheets. 'Personally, I don't actually think you're ready to go home but they don't have any choice. They don't have anywhere else to send you.'

She swept her arm across the ironing board to smooth out

the creases and then pushed the iron over the sheet, the steam rising up to obscure her face.

'But it's what I want,' I insisted. 'I want to live at home with my mum.'

'Aye, I ken that,' she sighed heavily, putting the iron back in the upright position and leaning heavily against the board. I was going to miss this – just sitting with Barbara in her kitchen while she ironed. It felt so normal, so secure.

She looked at me hard then: 'But that doesn't mean it's the best thing for you. Now, please, just try and stay in school as much as possible and no more going out getting drunk.'

'Aye, I promise,' I smiled. And at the time, I really meant it.

The problem was that nothing had changed at home – at least not in that sense. Mum was still drinking heavily, going on benders that lasted sometimes for three, four days or even a week. While I had been away, she'd had a little boy with her boyfriend Adam – it felt strange going into the house with a new baby but it didn't calm Mum down at all. She still went out all the time and Dionne would watch the baby while she wasn't there or when she'd had too much to drink. There were times we hardly saw her at all. My aunties popped in a lot just to check on us – and especially the baby. They'd ask if Mum was about and none of us knew the answer. She could be in the house, asleep in bed, and we'd never really know. More often than not, she was round at her boyfriend's place or one of the other friends she had in Armadale.

Jason was still around, though. The first time he told me to lie down for him after I got back from care, I refused. I told him I wasn't going to do it anymore. I had had a lovely break from him at Barbara's place and I realised that I had spent all that time protecting him when it didn't make any difference. I'd been sent into care anyway! So what right did he have to do these things to me when I didn't like it? I put my foot down.

'Nah!' I told him. 'I'm not doing it. I don't like it.'

'Aye, you will, you wee rat!' he growled. Then he launched himself at me and slammed me back down onto the floor, hurting the back of my head and my shoulders. He held me down with the full weight of his body and pulled my jeans off me, even as I squirmed and wriggled to stop him. He just pushed himself harder against me and when he finally got it inside, he did it really hard, just to hurt me.

After that I knew there was no point refusing. It was less painful to just let him get on with it. Around the others he acted like I didn't exist but when we were on our own, he made me do all those dirty horrible things that I hated. It made me so mad because Mum still thought he was the perfect child. He was still her 'golden boy' because he didn't cause any trouble. He didn't go out and get into fights or steal. He just liked to stay at home smoking hash, playing with his computer. Mum didn't mind that he was stoned all the time – at least it kept him quiet, she said.

It was lovely to see Dionne again but it felt like she didn't need me so much anymore. I guess she'd managed very well without me and in the time I'd been away, she'd become more independent, less clingy. She was the big sister now and she took up the role eagerly – feeding and changing Ollie, our little brother, and giving him his bottle. She was busy and she loved being in charge of the little one. Back home, it felt like I didn't belong anymore. Even my friends were getting on, doing their own thing. It was a shock – it felt like everyone had forgotten about me. Everyone, that is, except Jason.

For a while I kept up my good behaviour at school – I didn't want to get taken away again so I stayed in school and went home every day afterwards. I spent a lot of time with Dionne, taking her places, just to give my mum a break. I was careful not to take her anywhere near Bernie's or Pete's, though – instead, we went to the park or the shops.

One day I was messing around on the internet with Susan and we started chatting to these two boys – John and Simon, who were both fifteen. We arranged to meet up and we all got along really well. I liked John – not in a sexual way; I don't really know in what way I liked him. I just liked to hang out with him as a friend. One Saturday night, Mum was out drinking and she had arranged for a babysitter to stay in with us. I told the babysitter that my mum said I was allowed to stay at my friend's and I left a message for my mum telling her that that's what was happening. Then I went out to meet Susan and the boys at about 11pm.

My mum knew about John – she had picked up the phone when he called my house the week before.

'What's your name?' I heard her ask him sharply. I sensed this wasn't going to go well.

'And how old are you, John?' she inquired after a pause. Two seconds later she was screaming down the phone.

'What the fuck do you want with my daughter then? She's ten years old – did you know that? Ten! Don't ever fucking call here again, you bloody pervert! Leave my daughter alone!'

And with that she slammed down the phone.

It wasn't hard to convince him later when we spoke online that I was actually fourteen, not ten.

'That wasn't even ma mum,' I lied. 'I'm at college doing a hairdressing course right now.'

I knew that I wasn't old enough to be going out with boys but it hadn't stopped Jason, Pete and Bernie! After all these years, I didn't feel like a ten-year-old. I didn't relate to children my age. I had always felt older than that so I didn't see anything wrong with seeing John.

We were all having a lovely time, and it was just after midnight when we heard the banging on the door. Then a familiar screeching voice.

'Oh no!' I said. 'It's my mum.' At that everyone started to giggle in fear – everyone was a little scared of my mum.

She came storming up the stairs, went straight up to me and said: 'Which one is John?'

I pointed at him and she gave him a neat clip round the ear. He looked stunned and held his hand up to his head.

'She's ten years old!' she screamed, towering over him with her hands on her hips. 'I told you on the phone she's ten!'

'She told me she was fourteen,' he squealed, still hugging his ear, which was now red.

'Aye, well she's not!' Mum shot back. 'Are you stupid or something?'

'She told me...'

'Don't listen to her. I'm her mother and she's coming home!'

Then she picked me up by my hair and literally dragged me all the way back to our house.

'You're lucky I don't tell the social workers about this,' she stormed when she got me home that night. 'They'd take you away again for sure. Is that what you want?'

'No,' I said sullenly. It wasn't what I wanted at all. It just felt nice to be friends with a boy – someone who didn't do nasty things to me. But I couldn't tell that to Mum. There was so much I couldn't tell her.

It was June now and I was due to leave primary school for good. I didn't want to go. I loved going to school just so that I could play with Annie in the afternoons and I asked the headmistress if she'd let me come back to help out at the nursery once I moved up to secondary school.

'I'm sorry, Tressa, they're not going to allow you to do that,' she said.

So on the last day of term I had to say goodbye to Annie for good. And it was really sad. In the time I had known her it felt like we had become so close that she was almost like a sister to me. I stayed with her until her mum came to collect her at the end of the day. I recognised who she was the moment she walked in – she had the same white blonde hair and sky blue eyes. Annie ran towards her, her arms outstretched, and her mum swept her up in a warm embrace. Something clenched inside me then. Something tugged at my heart. Envy? Jealousy? Sadness? I didn't know. It was like a little painful jolt in my stomach and I felt like crying.

'Here you go,' I went towards them both, holding Annie's polka dot coat out for her. 'Don't forget to wrap up, Annie. It's cold out there... Brrrrrr!'

I made a pantomime of being cold, hugging myself and shaking my body. Annie laughed out loud.

Her mum looked at me questioningly and in another second, the penny dropped.

'Oh, so *you're* Tressa, then?' she asked, with a smile.

'Aye – I'm going up to the High School in September,' I said. 'I won't see Annie again.'

'I ken,' she nodded. 'She's going to miss you a lot. She talks about you all the time.'

'Really?' That made me smile. 'Does she really talk about me?'

'Aye, we know you've helped her a lot so thank you. Thank you for all you've done for her.'

'Och, it wasn't anything.' I suddenly felt shy, embarrassed. 'I've loved spending time with her. She's a beautiful little girl.'

'That's very kind of you to say,' her mum replied. By now Annie had climbed back down her mum and was fiddling with the knobs on the toy kitchen in the corner.

'Come on, Annie!' her mum called and then she put out her hand and little Annie took it.

'Bye Tressa,' she lisped in her little baby voice.

'Bye bye beautiful girl,' I whispered, barely able to hold back the tears. 'I'll miss you.'

'Miss you too,' she said and then her mum took her out of the nursery and it was finally time for me to leave. I wanted to stay there so much. In those seconds I would have given everything just to be able to stay in that nursery, safe, away from all the pain and troubles in the world. But it wasn't to be. I picked up my bag and my coat, and slowly followed her out. Life was changing again – too fast and too much.

I hoped I would be able to keep up.

CHAPTER 8

The Brickyard

'Tressa, we're going up to Edinburgh. You wanna come?' Alex asked me one humid August morning, as I lay sprawled out on the sofa watching daytime TV. It had been a long, boring summer so far and I spent most mornings in front of the TV. I tried to stay out of the sun as much as possible – I didn't enjoy the heat much and it was always nice and cool indoors. In the afternoons I usually took Dionne to the park and then, in the evenings, I hung out at my friend's house or by the shop. I still saw Peter and Bernie occasionally but I avoided going there if I was with Dionne. There was no way I could take her there.

Alex, Jason's pal, had been hanging around at our place that weekend with his other friend, Jason Barnes (JB), and they were in the kitchen with my friend Danielle. I had met JB once before when I had visited my brother Jason in a residential home. They were the same age and I remember he had been nice to me that one time – we'd played on the trampoline together and he'd shown me how to bounce onto my bottom and then back onto my feet again. JB was skinny, with dirty blonde hair and a mischievous smile.

'Aye, sure!' I replied. I didn't have anything better to do.

Just then Danielle wandered in, pulling her hair back into a ponytail as a fag dangled loosely from her mouth. She was fourteen but, like me, she seemed a lot older. Her eyes squinted against the smoke.

'But how we gonna get there?' I asked. None of us had any money.

'S'alright,' Danielle replied. 'I took some money from my ma's purse today. I got us thirty quid.'

'Aye, no bother,' I jumped to my feet. 'Just gi' us a minute to get ma coat.'

The four of us piled onto the train, laughing and joking. My brother Jason had been up late the night before on his computer and was still in bed when we left, so he stayed behind. It felt so good to be getting out of Armadale – since we never had any money, my mum never took us on holiday so just getting out for a day felt like a big adventure. Edinburgh was a big city, exciting and full of possibility! At the other end we jumped out and turned down Princes Street.

'Come on!' Danielle said, as we passed an off-licence. 'Let's get some booze. You go in, Alex. You look old enough!'

Alex came out with two large plastic bottles of cheap cider in a blue plastic bag.

'Good on yer!' JB cheered when he looked inside the bag. 'Let's go up by the Commonwealth Pool and drink it there.'

It was a long walk to the Pool and I fell into step next to JB. We started chatting then and it was nice to talk to him. He told me how he was still in residential but hated it. He was due to go back to his mum's place that night in Edinburgh.

'She's still a mess, though,' he sighed. 'I don't think I'll ever go back there for good.'

I understood what he meant – increasingly, Mum had gotten way out of control. One night I came downstairs and I found her smoking stuff off a piece of tinfoil through a little pipe. I knew what it was instantly: heroin. I'd felt sick at that moment. Until then I had no idea Mum was a drug addict. I'd heard rumours before, little things that people said to me, but I always dismissed them. Now I felt despairing about my mum. After everything we'd been through, it felt like she was throwing it all away. And for what? If the social workers found out she was using heroin as well, they would surely take us all away for good. I begged her that night to stop and she promised me she would.

'Aye, well, you never know!' I smiled up at JB. I didn't want him to feel bad.

'Yeah, you never know,' he muttered bitterly. But I could see he didn't have any real hope.

We got to the Commonwealth Pool and sat on the little grassy patch at the back, passing the bottles of cider between us, smoking and having a laugh. After a while we walked back to the shops and bought some chips and another two bottles of cider. We walked around a bit and then wandered back to the Commonwealth Pool. After that the day started to turn greyer and things got fuzzy. At some point JB said we should all go back to his mum's place – by then I was pretty drunk and I remember setting off for his place, but after that it all turned into a blur. BANG BANG BANG.

'Police – let us in!' The hammering on the door woke me immediately and I lay there for a second, wondering where I was and why I was naked. I looked about me. I didn't recognise anything in this strange room. I pulled the navy duvet around me against the early morning chill and then the bedroom door swung open.

A policeman was standing over me in the room. Just then I felt a movement behind me. It was JB! He leapt out of bed, half-dressed, and started babbling: 'What is it? What is it?'

I knew what it was – they were here for me. I'd known it the moment I'd heard the banging.

'Tressa Middleton?' the first officer asked me sternly.

'Aye,' I replied, rubbing my eyes.

'We've been trying to find you. Your mother reported you missing last night. Where have you been?'

'I've been here,' I replied nonchalantly. 'I had nowhere else to go.'

'Why did you run away?' the officer asked.

'I did nae run away,' I told him. 'I just went out with ma pals.'

By now JB had managed to get his T-shirt over his head and he was hopping round the room, pulling on his trainers. He looked guilty and frightened – personally, I was a little shocked to find myself naked in his bed. I could not remember if we had done anything the night before. But I wasn't scared. I was used to being picked up by the police by now.

'You need to come with us,' the police officer said to me, throwing a hard stare at JB.

'I need to get dressed first,' I said. I wasn't about to leap out of bed naked in front of this officer.

'Hmm, well, I cannae leave,' the officer said. He was clearly worried I'd try and escape out of the window but I told him I was too shy to get dressed in front of him.

'Please,' I begged. 'Just shut the door at least.'

So that's what he did – keeping the door open a little, ready to burst in if he heard anything strange. I dressed hurriedly, embarrassed now to be naked in front of JB. I needn't have worried – he was just pacing the floor, picking up bits of clothing, patting them down then discarding them again, muttering, 'Fuck, fuck, fuck' under his breath.

'What is it?' I asked.

'Can't find my fags,' he replied.

A couple of minutes later, Alex and Danielle came through to our room, escorted by another policeman. They both looked like they'd just been turfed out of bed – they wore sleepy, cross expressions and hair stuck up from all directions on their heads.

'You're to come with us, too,' the first policeman said to Danielle, as he walked in again. 'You've both been reported missing.'

They took us to the police station, and put Danielle and me into a holding cell. It was like an interview room but the door was open and a policeman sat outside it. Alex was in the room next door. Danielle and I just slumped on the chairs, both hungover and fed up.

'I don't want to go back,' she said after a while. 'I took my ma's money. She's going to kill me.'

'Aye, me too,' I said. And I wasn't wrong. The police dropped me back home later that morning and Mum was there, waiting at the door.

She thanked the policeman politely but as soon as the door closed behind us, she let rip.

'What do you think you're playing at?' she yelled. 'If you're going to keep this up, I'll have no choice. You'll be in care within the month!'

'You're only saying that because you don't want me here no more!' I shot back. 'You don't care. Anyway, you're never home. You'd prefer it if I was out of the way for good!'

It was true – Mum didn't work but then she was never home. So what was the point of me being there?

'They said that you were naked, Tressa!' she exploded. 'Naked in a boy's bed! I mean – Christ almighty! How do you think that looks to them? How do you think that'll affect your being here. I want you here but you're doing everything possible to get took off me again.'

'Och, nothing happened,' I waved my hand dismissively.

'Are you sure about that?'

'Aye, I'm sure.'

'He's a lot older than you, Tressa. If something happened, I need to know.'

'Trust me – nothing happened. Nothing!'

I knew for a fact that Mum would call the police if she thought we had slept together. After all, JB was fifteen. And in truth, I didn't know if anything had happened but I didn't want to get him into trouble. He was a nice enough lad.

From then on, I tried to stay out of trouble and not long after that, I started at Armadale High School. I was nervous at first – the place was huge, much larger than my primary school, and although I knew quite a few of the kids in my class from primary, there were a load more older kids there too. Luckily, I had caught up quite well from my final few months at primary school and by the time I started, I wasn't too far behind the rest of the class. I took my homework back each night and worked hard so that I managed to keep up with the others. It was nice to get out of the house, away from Jason, and it gave me something to do each day.

But best of all, I loved the art classes. We had a lovely teacher and she praised me a lot from the beginning.

'Aye, that's a beautiful drawing, Tressa!' she said admiringly as she stood behind me, her head tilted to one side, looking at my sketches of birds. 'You've got some talent there!'

Her words made me swell with pride. It wasn't often I was complimented on my work, much less for something I actually enjoyed. I loved using all the different materials and trying out new techniques. For a while, I lost myself in my creations, the same way I did when I was with Annie.

One Saturday afternoon in September I got in from taking Dionne to the park to find Jason sitting in the living room. It was like he was waiting for me because the moment I arrived, he leapt up and told me I had to go with him. Jason now had a girlfriend called Kate and he spent a lot of time around her place, which was a relief for me. But today he had that look in his eyes and I knew what he wanted.

'Uh-uh,' I said. 'I can't go. I've got homework.'

'Bollocks!' Jason replied. 'You're coming so don't argue.'

'Really, Jay, I can't today. I got to get this project done. It's got to be in on Monday.'

'Just shut up and follow me or you'll be sorry.'

And with that he stormed out the door. I sighed, told Dionne to watch TV while I was out and then followed him.

He marched ahead down the street in front of me and I struggled to keep up, jogging occasionally to match his long stride.

'Where are we going?' I called out.

'Brickyard,' he replied, not even turning to look at me. There was an old, abandoned brickyard about fifteen minutes' walk from our house. It had loads of old office buildings which lay empty, with their windows smashed up and chutes that came down from the top of the warehouse to the ground that were once used to carry the bricks. A lot of us kids used to go and play there when we had nothing better to do. There was no fence around it so we'd just go to hang around. In the middle of the yard was a large mound which had once been a huge pile of bricks, but the bricks had disintegrated over time and now it was just a big, sandy hill, good for climbing and BMX tricks.

Eventually, I caught up with Jason as we approached the brickyard. The air was getting colder now and big grey clouds loomed on the horizon. We wandered into the yard and Jason started to put his head into all the different abandoned offices, like he was checking to make sure there wasn't anyone about. I steeled myself. As long as he doesn't try to do it from behind again, I told myself, then it would be okay. I hated it that time. It was so painful and humiliating.

'Hey Tressa!' I heard Jason's voice calling me from inside one of the buildings. 'Come in here.'

I sighed, jammed my hands into my short pockets and followed the direction of his voice. I found him standing in the corner of one of the buildings, next to a bench.

'Come on!' he yelled impatiently. 'Hurry up!'

And I walked slightly faster towards him – no part of me wanted to be near him right now but I knew that if I resisted, it could be so much worse. So I went to him and as soon as I was there, he gestured for me to lie down on the bench. I did as I was told, then he pulled down my shorts to my ankles and he did the same.

He lay on top of me and I felt sick, lying there in that disgusting abandoned brickyard. He was a big lad now and the way he shoved me into the hard, stone bench was painful on my small, thin bones. He thrust into me again and again, and though I tried to make his thing go outside of me like it did that time when Alex caught us, it didn't work and he kept pushing it back inside until he was going so fast and then he came.

He pulled himself off me, without a word, and hitched up his jeans. Then he walked off, leaving me lying there. I sat up, slowly, feeling dirty and ashamed, and as I got to my feet, I felt the warm liquid from him dripping down the inside of my thigh and down to my legs. I looked about – there was nothing to wipe myself with. So I unhooked my shorts from my feet, took off my knickers and used those to wipe myself. Then I hurried out of the office building, the knickers balled in my hands. Jason was nowhere to be seen. The pale yellow light was fading now and orange streaked the sky. I had to get home for tea.

On the corner, I threw my knickers in a bin and got back in time to see that *X Factor* was on TV. Ollie was fast asleep in his bouncy chair and Dionne was at the table, tucking into a plate of fish fingers and chips.

'Tress, is that you?' Mum called from the kitchen.

'Aye,' I yelled back.

'Right – here you go,' she came through with a plate for me, puffing her cheeks out with the effort of moving about. She was heavily pregnant again – something I hated. She didn't have enough time for all the children she had already.

What was the point in having another one? When she'd told me, I went mad at her.

'Are we not enough for you?' I'd yelled at her. 'How many kids you gonna have? How many do you need? You're hardly here anyway to look after the ones you have got. It's not fair. You don't need any more babies.'

Mum had just rolled her eyes at me and walked off – she was used to my outbursts by now. In her mind, I was just being 'difficult' again. But I was honestly very angry with her. There wasn't enough of her to go round – there certainly wasn't enough for me!

Mum waddled towards me now, holding a plate of fish fingers and chips in one hand, and a bottle of ketchup in another.

'Get that down you,' she started to say. Then she stopped and looked at me.

'What?' I demanded. 'What is it?'

'I think you better get yourself cleaned up first. You been rolling in the mud or something?'

I looked down at my hands, arms and clothes – there were specks of mud and brick dust on my shorts and T-shirt. For a moment, my heart thudded and my face went hot with shame.

'I was at the brickyard,' I said quietly.

'Aye, well you're nae there now so wash yourself up a bit.'

I thudded upstairs and, before I went to the bathroom, I grabbed a pair of fresh knickers out of the laundry basket on the landing. I didn't cry anymore. There wasn't any point. This was my life now and there was no point getting upset. I put on the new knickers, washed my face and hands, and went back downstairs for my tea.

CHAPTER 9

Pregnant

The harsh smell of vinegar hit my nostrils and a second later, my stomach turned over.

'Urgh, I can't eat these!' I pushed my plate away. It was over two months later and Mum had gone to the chippy for our tea. But the moment she walked in with the bag of food, the waft of fried chips and vinegar made me feel sick. I'd been starving hungry just moments before but now I felt like throwing up. *Why was this happening? What was wrong with me?*

For the past two weeks I'd felt sick at the merest mention of food. I couldn't even think about eating breakfast without feeling the overwhelming urge to dive into the bathroom. And lately, I'd begun to experience weird pains in my abdomen. It was like period pains but my period refused to come. It had been two and a half months since that time with Jason in the brickyard and a tiny, scary thought crouched in the back of my mind, haunting my thoughts, keeping me awake at night.

Eventually, one day, when I was round at my friend Emily's place, I confided my fears.

'I think I might be pregnant,' I told her. 'I can't eat without feeling sick and I've got these funny pains in my stomach.'

'Really?' she said. 'Are you serious?'

'I don't know what else it could be,' I told her. I remembered how my mum had reacted to food when she was in the early months of pregnancy with Ollie. Now she had another little boy, Kai, who was still just a baby. It was the only thing that explained how I felt.

'Do you want to do the test?' she asked. I looked at her blankly.

'I think you better do the test,' she said, which made my mind up for me.

'How?' I said. I was too scared to go to the doctor's and terrified of telling my mum.

'My dad'll help you,' she said. Emily's dad was really cool – after Emily spoke to him, he didn't say anything to me. He just told us both to hop in the car and drove us round to Tesco's.

'Wait here, you two,' he said, as he opened the car door. 'I'll be back in a sec.' A few minutes later he got in the car and passed a chemist's bag to me over the backseat. Inside was a pregnancy test kit.

'Thanks,' I said in a small voice. It was embarrassing but I was grateful that he hadn't said anything to me. I didn't know what to tell him. When we got back, Emily and I went into her room and we opened the little box – I read the instructions and it said I had to wait until morning to do it. So I texted my mum and told her I was staying over at Emily's that night. She didn't mind.

PREGNANT

That night, I lay on the mattress on the floor beside Emily and my mind turned things over and over. *What if I was pregnant? What then?*

The next morning I almost forgot to do the test but then, just before I went into the bathroom, Emily called out to me: 'You going to take it in with you?'

'Oh right, yeah,' I shouted back. I couldn't believe I had left it there on the sideboard. I picked up the box and went to the toilet.

A few minutes later, I called Emily and asked her to come in.

'It's positive,' I said, my voice quivering with emotion. 'I'm pregnant.'

Emily let out a little nervous giggle, as her hand shot to her mouth.

'Shit!' she squeaked. 'What are you going to do?'

'I don't know,' I said.

'Your mum's going to kill you,' she breathed, eyes wide.

'I know,' I nodded. 'I'm not telling her.'

The rest of the day I went about as if I was in a dream. I couldn't quite believe it was true but the two blue lines had shot up straight away on the stick. There was no doubt about it: I was pregnant. It was a shocking thought – I was only eleven years old, barely out of primary school. What would people think of me? What would they say? They'd call me a slag, a whore. I hated the thought of all those people judging me. But I knew one thing for certain – this was Jason's baby. My brother Jason. I thought back to the brickyard. That was when it happened. And if I kept this baby then one day there would be proof – proof of what he did to me.

I was going to have this baby, I decided almost immediately.

Not because of Jason, but because I knew all babies loved their mothers and with that love, I would finally feel complete, secure and happy. I thought back to the day I saw Annie with her mother, the way she had leapt into her arms and the look of pure joy on her face to be reunited with the one person she loved best. Now I could have that too. I could have my own little baby who would love me above everyone else. And that baby would never leave me, never let me down and never let me go.

I walked home that afternoon in a daze, steeling myself for the inevitable row that I knew would come with my revelation. But I had to face this – I had to tell my mum. When I walked in, my aunty Joanne was in the living room.

'Where's Mum?' I asked her, flopping down on the sofa next to her.

'And hello to you too!' she replied tartly.

'Oh sorry,' I mumbled. 'Hello. How are you?'

'I'm fine, lovely. And how are you doing?'

'Not too good, actually,' I confessed.

'No?'

'No – I'm pregnant.'

A heard the sharp intake of air and then she said in a low voice: 'Oh. My. God. Seriously, Tressa?'

There was sadness in the question and in that second I realised I'd been holding my breath. I knew I wouldn't get this type of reaction from my mother.

'Mmmm-hmmm,' I nodded. 'I did the test this morning. Mum's gonna kill me. Where is she?'

'She's upstairs in the bath with Kai.'

'Will you tell her for me, Aunty Jo?' I begged. 'I can't do it. I really can't.'

She must have sensed my desperation because she blew out her cheeks then and pushed herself up off the sofa.

'Aye, I'll do it for you – but you better hide!'

I just sat there, staring at the TV, as Joanne climbed the stairs.

'You gonna hide?' she asked, as she got to the middle step.

I shook my head, still staring at the TV, unable to focus. I didn't really know what to do. I was rooted to the spot, my mind a blank.

I was still sitting there a few moments later when I heard the screams: 'SHE'S WHAT? YOU ARE FUCKING JOKING! I'LL KILL HER. I SWEAR TO GOD I'LL KILL HER.'

There was a splash, a heavy thud and then the wild pounding of feet coming down the stairs. My mum was wrapped in a towel, her hair was wet and flying about her head, and her face was beetroot red.

'YOU WEE BITCH!' she screeched as she flew down the stairs.

'Oh fuck!' I shouted as I sprang to my feet and headed for the door. In another second, I was through and out, running down the street.

Mum came after me, still wrapped in her towel, still screaming her head off: 'YEAH, YOU BETTER RUN, YOU WEE BITCH! I'M GOING TO KILL YOU. GET BACK HERE!'

I ran on, my heart now pounding in my chest, fear propelling me forwards until I found my friend Emily's door and I let myself in, quickly turning the lock behind me.

Mum was still outside: 'YOU BETTER HIDE, GOD DAMN YOU! YOU BETTER BLOODY HIDE, TRESSA, BECAUSE I WILL FIND YOU.'

Emily came down the stairs to find me panting and

dishevelled against her door, my mum's shouts still coming through from the street behind me.

'She lost it,' I burbled, my eyes now filling with tears of shock. 'She's gonna kill me.'

Emily just took my arm and led me to the kitchen, tutting and shaking her head: 'I told you. I told you so.'

I spent the next two hours at Emily's, nursing cups of tea and wondering whether I'd ever be allowed to go home again. She tried to calm me down but I was a mess, occasionally bursting out crying or sitting silently at the table, lost in my own little world.

Eventually, we heard the doorbell.

'It's all right,' my mother's voice called from the street. 'I'm alright now – I'm not going to go mental at you. I just want to talk. We've got to talk. We've got to sort this thing out.'

Emily went upstairs to her bedroom to get a look at my mum from her window.

'She's dressed now – she looks calm enough,' she told me when she got back. 'I think you better let her in.'

I didn't want to but I knew I'd have to face her at some point. So I hastily gulped down the last of my tea and went to the door.

'Come on,' Mum said when I opened it. 'Let's go home.'

'Whose is it?' she said after we got back to our place. We were in the living room together. Aunty Joanne had taken the little ones back to her place to give us some space to talk.

I didn't answer her.

'It's that Jason Barnes, isn't it?' she said. I didn't say a word – it was Jason all right. Just not the Jason she thought.

'Right, well, you'll have to have an abortion,' she said firmly, as if that decided the matter.

'No, I'm not,' I said in a small but equally firm voice.

'Aye you are!'

'Well, whatever,' I said. 'I know what I'm doing.'

Mum leaned forward now and spoke urgently. 'You're too young to be a mum. For heaven's sake – you're eleven years old. You're a baby! They'll never let you keep it.'

'It's not up to them and it's not up to you.'

'Right, whatever. I'm going to have to phone the social workers and tell them.'

'Why?' I said. I didn't want the social workers involved – what was it to do with them? I wanted this baby all to myself; I didn't want any of their meddling.

'Why do you think?' she said. 'They'll find out anyways. You're underage. Do you honestly think you can keep this a secret from them?'

Mum called the social workers, just like she said she would, and they made an appointment with me to visit the doctor. The pregnancy was confirmed and the doctor even listened to the heartbeat.

Later that day, they came to see us with the health visitor. At first, they asked to speak to Mum on her own, so I closed the door and went into the corridor. I stood there, with my ear to the door, listening to everything they said.

'Can't you make her?' I heard my mum saying. She sounded desperate.

'No, I'm sorry, Tracey,' June said. 'Because of her age we don't really have a say in it. It's her choice to keep the baby. We can't force her to have an abortion.'

'Aye, well if it were up to me, I'd hold her down and shove the bloody pill down her throat myself!' Mum retorted. 'She's too young for this!'

'And if you did that, Tracey, we'd have to arrest you for assault,' the social worker sighed. 'No, I'm sorry. We can't force her and neither can you.'

Relief washed over me then. None of them could take this baby away from me. It was my choice, my body, my baby.

'TRESSA!' My mum hollered. 'Tressa, you can come in now!'

I waited a few seconds before pushing the door open. I didn't want them thinking I'd been standing there the whole time, eavesdropping.

Mum gave me one of her narrow-eyed, mean stares as I sloped in to sit beside her. June was scribbling furiously in her file. The other social worker, Helen, looked at me and smiled with her mouth. Her eyes said something else.

'Tressa,' said Helen, folding her hands on her lap. 'We'd like to know what you want to do about the pregnancy.'

'I'm keeping it,' I said quickly. 'I want to keep the baby.'

'Are you sure about that?' she said slowly. 'Are you absolutely sure? You know this is a huge responsibility and obviously there will be repercussions.'

'Yes, I'm sure. I'm sure.'

She let out a long sigh then and June looked up from her writing. They exchanged resigned looks.

'Then it that case we can't take you away from your mum right now because it would be too stressful – for you and the baby. But, after the birth, well, you know what's going to happen, don't you?'

She meant I'd be taken off my mum. I knew she would

say this because Mum had told me the night before. It was considered neglect. Mum was already walking a tightrope with social services and now it looked like she'd fallen off altogether.

Mum crossed her legs and folded her arms, letting out an irritated sigh.

'We wouldn't really have a choice, Tressa,' Helen added. 'I mean, not unless things change around here.'

That gave me a small glimmer of hope – they might let me stay here after all! In my mind I felt confident that we could convince them everything would be fine and then after the baby was born, I could stay with Mum. Even if they wanted to take me into care, I had a plan to ask my aunty Marilyn to apply for custody of me and the baby. She had fostered for others before so I didn't see why it couldn't work.

So Mum resigned herself to the fact that I was now going to have a baby and although she didn't like it, and didn't talk to me for about a week afterwards, things went back to normal pretty quickly.

It was a few weeks later that I confronted my brother.

We were at a party for one of our cousins and I found him in a bedroom on his own, sitting on the end of the bed, one knee over his leg, skinning up a joint.

I closed the door behind me to drown out the loud whump of the house music.

'I'm pregnant, Jason,' I said, keeping my voice level.

'Yeah, I know,' he said, hardly looking up. He rolled the papers expertly with his thumbs and forefingers, then he stuck out his tongue and licked the edge to seal it.

'It's yours,' I added.

'I know. That's why you're not keeping it. You're going to get rid of it.'

He sounded so cocky again – just like all those times he made me lie down for him. But it wasn't going to work this time. He wasn't in control anymore.

'No I'm not,' I said calmly. 'I'm not doing anything with it.'

His eyes flicked up to meet mine as he carefully placed the thin end of the joint in his mouth. He put his head to one side, as if assessing me, working me out.

'Well, you know what you're going to do, don't you?' he spoke with the joint in his mouth, the fat end bouncing up and down in front of his face. 'Just remember – it'll be your fault if everybody gets took away and Mum gets put inside.'

He slid a lighter out of the pocket of his black hoodie.

'They won't get took away,' I told him confidently. He flicked the end of the lighter and it burst into flame. Then he held it to the end of the joint, which blazed into life. He let the flame die down and then he sucked hard, taking in a big lungful of smoke.

'Aye, well you know best,' he said, still holding the smoke inside his lungs. Then he blew the smoke out towards me and into my face. He smiled crookedly, and I turned and walked out.

I knew I was keeping this baby and that was the end of it. More than anything I wanted a little baby I could love with all my heart and hold in my arms. This child would never know hurt or pain the way I had, I vowed. I would protect it and keep it safe all the time. This child would know nothing but love and happiness in its life. I walked out of the party that day with my head held high. It didn't matter what anyone said. I knew everything was going to work out for the best.

CHAPTER 10

Pregrant... and the World Krows It!

'Waaah... Waaah.... Waaah... Waaah... Waaah...'
The strange, hiccupy wail from the corner of the room woke me instantly, and I rolled over and groaned.

'Waaah... Waaah.... Waaah... Waaah... Waaah...'

It was getting louder and angrier. On and on it went – I opened my eyes and tilted my head upwards to see my mum staring straight at me in her bed. It gave me a start.

'Waaah... Waaah.... Waaah... Waaah... Waaah...'

Oh Jesus – I knew what I had to do. I had to get up and sort Kai out. Mum had told me last night that if I wanted to have a baby, I'd have to prove that I could handle it.

'You want a bairn?' she'd said. 'If you want a baby, here, you've got one!' and she held Kai out to me.

'What do you want me to do?' I asked.

'Everything!' she shot back. 'Feed him, change him, get up

for him, comfort him, bathe him – the lot! You really want to be a mother? Here, you can practise right now.'

So from today it was me who was responsible for Kai. He was still just a few weeks old but Mum had said that she wasn't going to do anything for him at all. It would have to be me the whole way – which was why I was now sleeping in Mum's room instead of next door with my sister. The green numbers on the night clock read 2.23am – I looked at Mum again but she'd turned her back to me and was completely still under her duvet. This was up to me now.

So, reluctantly, I dragged my tired body out of bed and went over to the Moses basket.

'Here you go,' I soothed as I plucked him out of his sheets and patted his back. 'Come on, little man, let's go get you a bottle of milk.'

From that point on, Mum left me to cope with Kai on my own and she never lifted a finger for him. It was very hard work but I managed all right, though I was pleased to be able to get away to school in the week. It gave me a break from the wailing.

Word soon got out in our area that I was pregnant and people were gobsmacked. I felt ashamed walking to school each morning, my belly swelling under my school uniform, and I often caught people staring at me or whispering behind their hands. I tried not to let it get to me – at night, I'd lie in bed, stroking my belly and talking to the child growing inside me.

'Don't worry about what no one says,' I whispered to it. 'I'm not going to let anyone hurt you. I'll be with you forever. I promise.'

I didn't tell anyone the truth about the real father. I knew that if I did, Mum could have all of us taken away from her and it would break her heart if the two little boys were put into care. So I kept my mouth shut and tried to put it to the back of my mind.

Mum's 'test' lasted two weeks and though it was the most exhausting time of my life, I managed to look after Kai all by myself. I didn't complain once, though it was terrifying bathing him on my own. I knew that if I buckled under the pressure, Mum would start on at me again about having an abortion so I just got on with it. The school was told very early on and they agreed to support me during my pregnancy for as long as they felt it was safe. I was really pleased about that because I enjoyed going to school. The only problem was some of the other kids. There was an older boy called Tom who lived not far from me and who had started bullying me; when he found out I was going to have a baby, it just got worse.

At first it was just name-calling. He would shout out 'Dafty!' and 'Idiot' to me in the street. He liked to try and rile me by calling my mum a junkie, which made me so mad. Whenever anyone said anything about my mum, I went mental. At school Tom and his friends would follow me around in the corridors, talking about me loudly, and then when I turned around, they'd all start laughing. It was really stupid stuff but it made me so angry.

One day after school, I was doing a sponsor sheet for charity with Dionne and we went round all the houses in our street, trying to get names. When we got to Tom's house, Dionne insisted we ring the bell.

'Nah,' I said. 'Let's leave this one.'

'No, I want to get more sponsors!' she said and before I had a chance to reply, she rang the bell.

Tom leaned out of the upstairs window and when he asked what we wanted, Dionne told him.

'It's a sponsored walk for charity!' she shouted cheerfully, waving the sheet over her head.

'Oh right,' he replied. 'I'll go get my ma for yous.'

Then he disappeared.

I had a bad feeling about this so I tapped Dionne on the back and said, 'Come on, let's go.'

'No, let's wait,' she replied.

A minute later Tom reappeared at the top window with a strange smirk on his face.

'Look up!' he called.

'What is it?' I asked, craning my neck to look at him, and that's when he poured it over us. At first I thought it was just water but within seconds the smell hit me and I realised it was urine. It was still warm. We ran home that day and jumped in the bath. It was horrible.

Everything came to a head a week later in school. Tom had been following me again and I'd just got to the steps outside the school door when I turned around and he shoved me.

I thought I was going to fall! For a second I teetered on the edge of the step, twirling my arms around to balance myself, but thankfully I managed to stay upright.

The bastard! I saw red – *I was pregnant!*

Without thinking, I swung at him and landed a hard punch in his stomach. He retaliated and then we were proper brawling together. The headmaster came out just in time to see me slug

Tom again, full in the face. And that's when I got expelled. The headmaster said I had attacked Tom and even though I didn't see it that way, I was relieved not to be going back there. As long as he was still in that school, I didn't feel safe.

So now I was home more with Mum, helping her look after the little ones, and as the months passed, and I turned twelve, I marvelled at the changes in my body. I loved pressing my hands against my tummy and feeling the little kicks from the baby inside.

'Aye, you're a wee fighter, aren't you?' I'd smile as the baby punched and kicked me from within. 'Just like your ma!'

I spent a lot of time with Ollie, taking him swimming and to the playground. We became very close. On the way up to the pool every day, I'd let him sit on my bump and every time he'd shout: 'Baby's kicking my bum!'

In the afternoons, we'd watch CBeebies together and he'd lie with his head on my tummy, talking and listening to my belly. Then, when its little foot kicked me and we could see the imprint of its toes on my skin, Ollie would laugh and shout out: 'Bad baby!'

I loved Ollie so much – after a while, it felt like he was mine. I imagined I was carrying a little boy too but I didn't know for certain. And I tried not to think about the baby's relationship to Ollie. He was both his uncle and his brother. It made my head go funny.

One morning in April I was helping Mum hang up the washing on the line when a very pretty woman with long blonde hair, and wearing a smart black skirt and a white shirt, approached our house.

'Excuse me,' she asked, 'is there a Tressa living here?'

Mum eyed her suspiciously: 'Who are you?'

'My name is Gail Cameron. I'm a reporter for the *Scottish Sun*,' she replied, smiling. She had on beautiful make-up and I guessed she must be in her late twenties. She slung her large black handbag over her shoulder and walked towards us, confidently holding out a hand to shake. Her heels clacked loudly on the pavement as she got closer.

'Fuck off!' Mum said angrily. 'Go on – get away from my door and fuck off!' Then she shot me a look and waved her hand behind her back, which I knew meant she wanted me to get behind her. I crept towards her – I didn't know what this was about.

Gail seemed undeterred.

'Are you Tracey?' she asked sweetly. 'I was wondering if I could speak to you. It's just that we had a phone call – somebody phoned in and said that there was a wee girl here called Tressa. She's eleven and she's pregnant.'

'That's shite! Now go away!'

With that, Mum took me by the hand and led me back into the house.

My bump was very big now and because I was so skinny, it stuck right out in front of me.

As we passed, Gail tilted her head to one side and said to me: 'So, you're not pregnant then?'

Cheeky cow, I thought.

'I'm not eleven,' I snapped back and walked inside.

It had never occurred to me that the press would be interested in me. Why would they? It was strange that this woman had just turned up at our door. Who had told her about me?

'We'll pay you for your story,' Gail called out after us.

'We don't want your money,' Mum shouted over her shoulder. 'Go away!'

'Here, take my card, just in case you change your mind,' said Gail. 'We are going to run the story so you either talk to us and we pay you or we write it ourselves and pay the person who gave us the information. Either have your say or read what other people have to say.'

My mum stopped for a second, turned round and whipped the card from Gail. Then she followed me inside, slamming the door behind her.

Later, Aunty Marilyn and Aunty Joanne came round for a cup of tea and a chat. Mum was spitting mad – she told them about the reporter, Gail, and how she had threatened to run the story about me.

'I know who's done this,' Mum raged. 'It's that bloody Pamela from across the street. She's had it in for me for ages. Do you know her? She's a right bitch.'

Aunty Joanne was flipping the card over and over on the table.

She looked at Mum: 'Do you really think they'll do the story anyway?'

'Aye, that's what she said,' said Mum, lighting a fag.

'Well, maybe you should do it then,' said Aunty Joanne thoughtfully.

There was a silence. I stood at the window, looking into the back garden, watching the fresh buds on the trees beyond our back gate swaying in the breeze. The monotonous whirr of the washing machine next to me filled the room.

'What did she say about money?' I asked, still staring at the trees outside.

'You get paid,' my mum said, 'for every story that you give to the papers. They pay you.'

'How much do you get?' I said.

'It depends.'

Another silence.

Then Mum said quietly, 'Think what we could do with that money. We could get the house done up. We could get your room ready. We could get stuff for the baby.'

I turned to face her then: 'What are you thinking, like?'

'Well, I'm thinking maybe we should do it.'

Half an hour later Mum called Gail on her mobile. It was a short conversation and thirty seconds later the doorbell rang.

'It's her,' said Mum. 'She never left. She's been sitting outside in her car the whole time with a photographer.'

Gail came in, followed by a man in a leather jacket with two very large cameras slung over each shoulder. Gail introduced me to him and, after a quick chat with Mum, she said I should go outside with the photographer to take the picture.

I was wearing a black skirt with a white line going around the top and my flowery top was tight across my belly.

The photographer asked me to pull my top up a bit and my skirt down so he could see my full bump and then he started snapping away.

After a bit we went inside and Gail asked me loads of questions about who the father was and how it happened. I told them what I told everybody else – that it was Jason Barnes and that I'd got drunk and we'd had sex without a condom.

She asked me how I felt about being pregnant, what happened when I found out and whether I was looking forward to it. We got talking about what we'd done to prepare for the baby and I told her all about looking after my wee brothers.

It went on and on – I couldn't believe ordinary people would be interested in this sort of stuff. I thought only celebrities went into the papers.

After they left, I didn't think much of it and the rest of the day passed normally. But the next morning when we opened the curtains we saw Gail and her photographer sitting outside the house in their car again.

'What are you lot doing here?' Mum called out when she opened the front door. Gail opened the car door and came trotting up to meet Mum in her tall black heels.

'We think you may have some other visitors today,' Gail said breathlessly. 'Maybe the *Daily Record* or the *Daily Mail*.'

'Why?' said Mum.

'Well, the story's gone in the paper today and of course we didn't pay the other woman for it because we got it directly from you so I wouldn't be surprised if she calls the other papers to try and get money from them.'

'Oh right,' Mum said, not really that bothered. 'Well, have you got the paper? Are you going to show it to us then?'

Gail fished out a copy of *The Sun* from her large handbag and I was shocked to see the picture of me in the front garden right on the front page. Only my face was blurry. Gail had told me the day before that, because of my age, they couldn't name or picture me. But still, I never imagined they'd put my story on the front page. I was horrified.

'Oh my God!' I exclaimed. 'Oh my God, oh my God!'

The way the photographer had made me pull down my skirt and pull up my top made it look like my clothes were too tight!

Mum took the paper from Gail and we all went inside the house to read it. We all stood round Mum at the kitchen table, reading the story in silence.

After a while, Mum sat back and looked at Gail. 'Yeah, that's not too bad,' she murmured. I was reading over her shoulder. My cheeks were red with embarrassment. There were some bits in there I really didn't like at all – the way it called my mum 'Granny' and how it said she was proud of me. That wasn't true – Mum had been furious when she'd found out I was pregnant. Also, they made a really big deal out of me smoking. I knew it wasn't a good thing but I'd tried to give up and failed. The way it was worded, it made me sound like a slag and I was afraid that people would turn against me when they read it. Even though my name wasn't mentioned, everyone who knew me would recognise it was me in the paper.

'My editor loves the story!' Gail raved. 'He thought you were both brilliant and that's why it went onto the front page. But of course, there'll be others interested in what you have to say so that's why I'm going to stick around today and make sure they don't bother you none.'

Mum's eyes were on Gail now. I could see she was already thinking ahead. She turned around and walked over to the kitchen sink without saying a word. There was a long silence.

Then, with her back still turned to Gail, she started: 'So, if you don't want anyone else getting the story, does that mean you'll have to pay us more? I mean, if we decided we *wanted* to talk to the *Daily Mail*, we could get money from them too, couldn't we?'

'Ur, eh…' Gail hesitated. 'Well, I'll have to talk to my editor about that.'

'Aye, you do that,' Mum said. She picked up her pack of fags, tipped one into her hand and put it in her mouth. 'You do that, Gail.'

From that day on, Gail practically moved in with us. She was in our house almost all the time and when she wasn't tapping on her laptop, she would watch TV with us or talk round the kitchen table. I hated all the attention – even though the story had been anonymous because I was so young, all the people in our area knew it was me, and people started looking at me differently after I appeared in the paper. Even the shopkeeper at the end of our street would talk to me when I went to buy milk.

'Are you going to be in the paper in the morning?' he'd ask, with a sly wink. 'You want to give me the heads-up so I can get more in? You're selling loads of papers for me!'

There were comments in the street now – nasty comments – and even a couple of my good friends turned on me.

'Don't take any notice of them,' Mum said after a particularly bruising fight with Danielle. 'She's just jealous because we're getting all the money.'

'It's not that,' I sulked. In fact, Danielle had slagged off my mum more than me – she said my mum was a useless junkie and that's why I got pregnant. What she said about me didn't bother me – but I wasn't going to have her bad-mouthing my mother.

The other consequence of my pregnancy being in the papers was that the police were forced to do something about it. They arrested JB and charged him with underage sex – something I felt bad about. After all, I didn't want to get anyone into trouble. My brother Jason didn't like the attention either; he complained about Gail being in the house all the time and said that people kept hassling him about his pregnant sister. The one nice thing about being pregnant was that Jason left me alone – but I could tell he was uncomfortable with all the attention on us, so I did my best to reassure him.

'You don't have to worry,' I said to him one day when we were alone in the kitchen. 'I'm not going to tell anybody. I won't say a word.'

'Good,' he replied and walked out.

As the pregnancy progressed, I got more and more nervous about the birth – I'd heard it could be really painful and I'd wake up in the middle of the night, shaking and sweating from horrific nightmares where the baby came out stillborn. I was shown round the hospital beforehand and they explained that if I was in a lot of pain, they could give me an epidural which would make my whole body go numb so I wouldn't feel anything. I asked them what an epidural was and that's when they showed me the needle. Oh my God, it was gigantic! I nearly fainted just looking at it – so that didn't help my fears at all.

About a month before my due date, I went for a check-up with my health visitor and she said the baby was looking a bit small, so I was sent up to hospital for a scan.

It was then that they told me I was expecting a girl.

I was so excited I dashed home and told everyone. Mum didn't seem that bothered but when I saw Gail, she was really happy for me. I loved the idea of having a wee baby girl.

'I'm going to see if we can help you out,' Gail smiled, picked up her mobile and phoned her editor. After she got off the phone, she grinned: 'He says you can have £500 to get baby stuff!'

I squealed with delight. It was lovely to be able to buy all new clothes and babygros for my daughter. After all, we only had boy stuff in our house. I went out and bought loads of stuff, and it brought a big smile to my face that night, holding it all up and folding it away in the drawers.

It wasn't long now, just a few weeks to go. I was excited but also so scared – and the one thing that scared me most was the thought that my mum wouldn't be around to help me. Her drinking was worse than it had ever been and there were times I'd wake up in the middle of the night to go to the bathroom and caught her smoking heroin.

'MUM!' I'd scream. 'You promised me you'd stop that stuff! You promised!'

'Oh Christ, Tressa, it's just a wee bit – calm down!'

'But you said you'd stop for me and for the baby!' I felt desperate now. The social workers had said that if things changed then maybe we wouldn't get taken away after the birth and I was depending on Mum to stay clean so that I got to come home with the baby. I wondered about all the money from Gail. At first, I had had some money put into my bank account but after that, all the payments from the press went straight to my mum. I could see where the extra cash was going.

'What if they find out?' I pleaded with her.

'Aye no bother,' Mum drawled now, her eyes half-closed, her voice brought low and soft by the powerful drug. 'It'll be alright. Don't worry, Tressa. It'll be fine. It'll all be fine.'

CHAPTER 11

Arrie

The newly cleaned windows sparkled in the hazy summer sunshine. I listened to the tinny whirr of the vacuum cleaner as I pushed it around my room. I was getting ready for this baby, my baby, and I wanted my room to be just right. But all the while a terrible thought dragged at the corners of my mind, refusing to go away, until I sat down on the bed and gave in to my fears.

It was 9am on 13 June, the day before my due date, and Mum hadn't come back the night before. I'd barely slept for worrying. Aunty Joanne had been over for the last two days, looking after the young ones, and she kept trying to reassure me that my mum would never let me down, but I was fuming. *Why did she have to do it? Why did she abandon me just when I needed her most?* Lately, she'd been worse than I'd ever known. I hardly saw her these days and when I did, she was usually drunk.

I loved my mum more than anybody in the world; I loved her. And yet, I never really understood her. *Why did she have all these children if she didn't want to take care of them? Why did she keep smoking kit – that's what everyone called heroin around here – when it threatened her chances of keeping her kids? What was it about life that she found so difficult?* I knew she'd had a hard upbringing herself – my granny had her own demons and issues that made life tough for my mum, four aunties and two uncles. They were involved with social services from a young age because they were often off school and out of control. But it seemed that Mum hadn't learned anything from her childhood – she just kept making the same mistakes.

A couple of weeks earlier, I caught Mum smoking kit in the bedroom with Ollie and Kai in there. She was there with her new boyfriend, Gareth, a man I disliked from the moment I set eyes on him. I knew he was trouble – he was a drug addict and it looked like he was dragging my mum down with him. I knew all the money from the stories we sold to *The Sun* was going up in smoke. But to find her smoking in front of wee 'uns... It was too much.

'Get out!' I screamed at Gareth.

'It's nae your place to tell him to go,' Mum shouted back at me.

'You're smoking kit in front of ma wee brothers,' I shot back. 'I think I've got a pretty good say in what happens around here. This is our house as well, not just yours!'

'This is ma house,' she said in a low, menacing voice. 'And I'll say what goes and what doesnae.'

It ended badly – I picked up an ashtray and threw it at

Gareth, and then he grabbed me by the hands and spun me round, pinning me to the bed. Jason rushed through when he heard my screams and pushed him off me. Then I went to my aunty Marilyn's house, where I reported Gareth to the police. I was fuming – what right did he have to assault me like that? Mum was so angry with me but at that point I didn't care – I wished the social services would come and take us all away from her.

I got up again – it didn't do any good to just sit there, worrying. I packed up the vacuum cleaner, winding the cord slowly round the handle at the back, and set about cleaning out my drawers. I had to do something – it was killing me not knowing where Mum was. She was my birthing partner. I didn't want to go through this without her. Yet, with every day that passed it felt like I was more and more alone.

When I heard her key turn in the door, my body tensed with expectation. I pushed myself up from where I was kneeling on the floor and felt the familiar twinge on my thighs. For the last two weeks the baby had been lying on a nerve which sent sharp little shooting pains down my legs. There were times I couldn't even walk for the pain. I eased myself to my feet and waddled heavily down the stairs. Her coat was slung casually over the back of the armchair, and in the kitchen Mum was making herself a cup of tea, acting like everything was fine. I seethed.

Didn't she care about us? It felt like she put Gareth first these days and all of us – her kids – second.

'I hope you're happy,' I said through gritted teeth, as the pain shot up my leg and through my spine.

She just ignored me while she buttered herself some toast.

I sat down in the living room with Dionne, who was watching TV, and tried to concentrate on *This Morning*, where they were giving a cookery demonstration. Aunty Joanne was in another room with the little ones.

'And on a medium heat, just give the onions a quick browning...' the chef was saying, shaking the pan in front of him.

She doesn't care! I fumed silently to myself. *She just doesn't care about me or my baby. She only wants to get out of her head all the time.*

'Then add the chicken and the garlic...' The chef was now pouring a small bowl of chicken pieces into the pan, causing the oil to sizzle and spit.

'And just make sure you've browned off the chicken before adding your chopped vegetables...'

OW!

Jesus Christ!

A sharp stabbing pain shot up my belly. *This bloody baby must be back on my nerve again*, I thought, as I flinched against the powerful spasm.

I tried to concentrate on the programme again but a second later the pain went through me again, this time harder, taking my breath away.

'Just give it a very quick flash fry...' the chef carried on jovially, now flipping the pan so the ingredients leapt up and sank back in a different place.

'Ahhh!' I winced as the pain gripped me again. At that moment Mum wandered back into the living room.

'What is it?' Mum asked, concerned.

'Ah nothing,' I replied, annoyed. 'I just got a sharp pain. That's all.'

Mum creased her brows then and looked at me hard: 'How long has that been going on for?'

'I don't know,' I replied testily. 'About half an hour. It's Braxton Hicks – that's what the midwife said last… Ow, fuck!'

A wave of pain hit me again and I doubled over in agony.

'That's nae Braxton Hicks,' Mum said levelly. 'That's labour, darling. You're having contractions. We'll have to go to the hospital.'

'What? *Now?*' I asked in a small voice. I was scared. *Was the baby really coming now?* I wasn't ready for this.

'Aye, now,' Mum said calmly. 'Don't worry – I'll call your aunty Marilyn and we'll both go with you.'

Moments before I'd been furious with her but all that evaporated in a second – I needed my mum more than anything now. I went upstairs, bracing myself against the pains, which were coming harder and faster now, grabbed my hospital bag and all my paperwork, and waited for our lift to arrive. As we waited, Mum texted Gail to let her know what was happening.

It was 11am when we got to the hospital and, at first, everything seemed fine. Despite my fear of the needle, I was more frightened of the labour pains so at noon they gave me an epidural and from there, I felt a little bit more relaxed as the whole of my bottom half went numb. Mum and Aunty Marilyn stayed with me in the birthing suite and the nurses came in every hour or so to check on how I was progressing.

The time ticked slowly by – I lay on the bed, unable to feel my legs or anything below my waist, increasingly anxious. Mum and Marilyn flicked on the TV and settled down to watch the afternoon soaps – but I couldn't concentrate. I put my earphones on and listened to my music, hoping that this would calm me down. At 7pm my dad came in with a bunch of flowers and a little pink babygro for the baby.

'Thanks, Dad,' I smiled weakly.

'You're not supposed to give her nothing till after the baby comes,' Mum snapped at him.

'Aye, well, no harm done,' my dad said. He didn't stay long, and afterwards, I felt restless and impatient. The nurse came back in – I was still only four centimetres dilated.

'I've been here hours already,' I said to my mum. 'Why isn't the baby coming?'

'Och, it's just slow because she's your first,' Mum soothed, taking my hand in hers. 'Don't you worry. It'll all be fine.'

At midnight Gail came in to see how I was. It was lovely to see her – by now Gail and I had become really close and I felt that she was on my side. As she left, she handed my mum some cash and told her it was to get stuff for the baby – a cot, clothes, that sort of thing.

By now, I could feel some of the pain returning to my legs and belly. The epidural was wearing off and as each minute passed, it seemed to get worse and worse.

'Oh God!' I panted, doubling over in agony. 'Oh God... Nngggggggg!' I clamped my mouth shut to stop myself from screaming but my whole head started to shake and it felt like I was being swept away in a tidal wave of pain.

In the short break between the pains, I begged Mum to find the nurses so they could top up the epidural.

Half an hour later and I was still in agony.

'I can't find anybody!' Mum looked wild-eyed and

desperate. 'I've asked the lady on reception and she says she'll send somebody when they're free. But she says it could be a while.'

'OW! JESUS! OH GOD, OH GOD, OH GOD!' I was shaking and shivering now but I couldn't move my legs so I just lay there, crying and screaming.

'We've got to get her something,' Aunty Marilyn gibbered next to me as I writhed around in the bed. It felt like I had slipped into another plane of reality, another world where all I could do was feel. I couldn't speak, hear or see and I could hardly focus on what was going on in the room. Somewhere out there, I knew my mum and aunty were trying to help me but I couldn't communicate anymore; I felt helpless, paralysed by the pain. Nobody had told me it would be like this! I didn't want this! I wanted to go home.

'I've tried,' Mum said, frustration and anger leaking out of every word. 'They keep saying they'll find somebody. I don't know what else to do!'

'I'll go!' I heard my aunty say firmly from somewhere far away.

The next couple of hours were horrendous – the pain was unbearable but when the nurses finally arrived, I was already 10 centimetres dilated and the baby's heartbeat was dropping. Mum held my hand the whole time, comforting me and telling me how well I was doing.

There was now a real sense of panic in the room as the midwives and nurses rushed about.

'We'll have to get her out now, Tressa,' said one of the nurses. I started to whimper.

'I can't. I can't. I'm so tired.'

'Don't worry,' I heard my mum's voice, calm and reassuring. 'It's going to be fine. Everything is going to be fine. You just have to start pushing.'

But I could barely keep my eyes open at this point – the pain had drained me of all my energy. A wave of nausea slid up my throat and I gagged. Oh Christ! I needed to sit up to stop myself choking on my vomit but I couldn't because they had my legs up in the stirrups. I tried to push myself up from the bed but I felt firm hands pushing me back down again. Were they trying to kill me?

'I'm gonna be sick!' I managed to yell before turning my face to the side to vomit. A nurse dashed to my side to mop it up. I fell back down on my back, crying.

'You have to push now, Tressa,' the midwife said.

'No, I don't want to,' I wailed. 'I want to go home.'

'Come on now, Tressa!' Mum urged. 'You can do this. You need to do this for the baby. PUSH!'

'Heartbeat's dropping,' said one midwife who had been monitoring the machine attached to the baby's head.

'What?' Fear gripped me and I looked at my mum. 'What's she saying? Is the baby alright?'

'Yes but you have to push, Tressa. You can do this. I know you can. For the baby. You're doing really well. Just push. PUSH!'

But I was exhausted and the pain was unbearable. I was a wreck. At some point I was given an injection down below for the pain but it was too late; I felt everything.

'She won't get her out.' I heard the voice of the doctor now. 'We're going to need the suction.'

Somebody passed him the suction cap – I was sweating

and aching all over, then I felt a sharp stinging sensation down below.

But finally I heard a cry and in that moment I burst into tears. My baby! My baby!

I reached out my arms – I needed to see her, to feel her. The nurse gave her a quick check and then passed her to me, wrapped in a towel. I looked down at her tiny little face, all scrunched up, and the strange conical shape of her head from the suction, and I could hardly believe this was real. She was exquisite, delicate and light as a feather.

'Oh, hello!' I whimpered, tears streaming down my cheeks. I couldn't believe she was here – she was mine.

'Congratulations, Tressa,' the midwife beamed. 'A beautiful, healthy baby girl. She's 6 lb 14 oz. Have you got a name?'

'Yes, she's called Annie,' I smiled weakly. It was 2.47am – I'd been in labour for sixteen hours and I was practically delirious from exhaustion.

I looked up at my mum and she beamed back at me.

'I'm so proud of you,' she said, tears springing to her eyes. 'Look at her – she's beautiful.'

She really was: those tiny eyes, the little wrinkled fingers pressed together in a tight grip. I stroked the top of her head. The nurses and doctors were bustling about, packing up the machines. I looked down again – I couldn't see her breathing. Why wasn't she breathing? Something was wrong. I just knew it.

'She's not breathing,' I whispered. Nobody took any notice.

'She's not breathing!' I said again, louder this time.

The nurse hardly looked in my direction when she replied: 'Och, she's fine. She's fine.'

But I looked into her face again and now I saw that she was turning blue.

'No, she's not breathing!' I was angry now. *Why weren't they listening to me?* 'She's blue. Look at her!'

My little girl had turned a strange ashen colour and her body was starting to go limp in my arms but nobody seemed to be paying me any attention so I started screaming: 'She's blue! Look at her! She's not moving!'

At that moment a nurse came towards me, looking as though she was going to try and reassure me. I shoved out my arms and practically threw my baby at her.

'LOOK AT HER!' I screamed.

Everything then seemed to happen in slow motion: I registered the shocked look on the nurse's face, the doctor spinning round and looking horrified, and then all the nurses dashing towards my daughter.

My little girl disappeared from my sight and I was overcome with panic.

'WHERE IS SHE? WHERE ARE THEY TAKING HER?' I shouted. My mum shook her head, unable to reply. My aunty Marilyn leapt to my side to offer me a comforting hand but I was beside myself now, gripped by a panic worse than any pain I'd experienced.

'WHERE'S MY BABY?' I screamed over and over again. 'WHERE'S MY BABY?'

I was panting hard now, unable to catch my breath, and I felt myself thrashing around, trying desperately to get off the bed. Just then I saw the doctor looking over me, a large needle in his hands.

'WHERE'S MY BABY?' I yelled desperately, tears soaking

my cheeks. He put the needle into my arm, and the next minute I felt my whole body relax and my mind start to swim away from me. The last thing I remember was looking into Aunty Marilyn's worried blue eyes – and then it all went dark.

'Tressa!' I heard my name through the depths of my slumber and slowly pulled myself to the surface of consciousness. I blinked and for a moment I couldn't focus. I blinked again.

I was in a hospital ward and my eyes fell on my mum and my aunty Marilyn.

'Tressa!' Mum was shaking me now and suddenly it all came back to me. My eyes snapped open.

'My baby! Annie! Where's Annie?' I asked groggily. As I came to, I noticed that there were nurses and a doctor standing at the end of my bed.

'Tressa, Annie's really ill and she's being transferred,' Mum said slowly.

'I want to see her,' I jumped in.

Now the doctor spoke: 'You can see her before she goes in the ambulance. Then we'll transfer you too.'

'What's wrong with her?' I asked, scared to hear the answer. Tears threatened to overwhelm me but I tried to hold them back. I had to keep it together for Annie's sake.

'It's her lungs,' the doctor said. 'They're underdeveloped. She'll go through to the Little France Hospital in Edinburgh, where they have a specialist unit to take care of her. Tressa, she's in a critical condition.'

I tried to take in what he was telling me but the words just refused to go in – all I wanted at that moment was to see my little girl.

It was early morning – about 6am – and a wheelchair was produced by my bedside. I was helped out of bed and lowered into the chair. I could feel a low throbbing pain coming from down below but I didn't care. I was wheeled out of the ward by the nurse and through two sets of double doors – then she used her electronic key to get us into the ward with all the incubators. As soon as I saw Annie, my vision began to swim, as the tears came again. She was so tiny, and she had tubes attached to her nose and mouth, as well as pads on her little chest. My heart broke.

'Oh my beautiful angel!' I whispered, putting my fingers to the Perspex dome. She looked so fragile, so helpless. I wanted to reach in and touch her, to hold her in my arms, but the nurse told me she was too weak to be moved. I just sat there for ages, staring at her, willing her to get better.

'You're a little fighter,' I told her. 'Remember that, Annie. Don't give up! You'll get through this.'

Then I sank back in the wheelchair and the nurse wheeled me back to my room.

'Do you want some help getting yourself cleaned up?' she asked. I didn't know what she meant at first but then I looked down at myself and saw I was still covered in dried brown blood.

I shook my head.

'It's okay,' I told her. 'I'll be fine on my own.'

She left me then and, very gently, I pushed myself up out of the chair. My legs felt like jelly. It was like I had forgotten how to use them. I tried to limp to the bathroom but halfway there my legs gave up and I fell to the floor. By now everyone had left so I just used my arms to slide myself along the floor the rest of the way and used the door frame to push myself back onto my feet. By the time I'd finished showering, I could walk a little better. But by then the painkillers had worn off and I was in agony all over again. I pressed the buzzer to call the nurse.

'They're taking Annie in an ambulance now,' said the nurse when she came in. 'We'll get you there soon, okay?'

The kindness in her eyes nearly killed me. I was scared, overwhelmed and confused all at once.

'Is it my fault?' I asked her in a tiny voice. 'Did I do that to her?'

'No,' she said gently. 'Not at all, Tressa. Don't blame yourself. She's just a poorly little girl. But don't worry. You'll be with her soon enough.'

CHAPTER 12

The Choice

I stared in wonder at the tiny body in front of me. *Had I really given birth to this baby? Was I really a mother?* It seemed so strange, so unreal – yet here she was. Now we were in the Little France Hospital in Edinburgh, I had all the time in the world to look at her, to examine every part of her – and I drank her in. I marvelled at her perfect little feet, the tiny nails on the end of each toe like drops of water. I looked into her face, admiring the puffed out cheeks and delicate eyelashes. She was so perfect it took my breath away.

It took a couple of days before her lungs were strong enough to come off the ventilator and the first time I got to hold her was magical. She was so light. I pressed my face to hers and felt the silky touch of her new skin on mine. I breathed in her milky, clean scent and touched the soft, frizzy brown tufts of hair on her head.

'You're beautiful,' I whispered, smiling. 'You're just so beautiful.'

I knew I wanted to be with her forever, to protect her and keep her safe. I spent every moment I could by her side and in the middle of the night, when she woke up crying, the nurses came to get me to help settle her. I went every time and though I wasn't always successful, I tried my best, whispering to her and stroking her arms. I was desperate to bond with her, for her to recognise me as her mum, but it was so hard with her being in intensive care.

There, in the unit, we only had two passes for relatives to come and visit. Mum and Aunty Marilyn visited frequently but Ollie and Kai weren't allowed in because they had colds and the babies in the ward were so vulnerable that even a cold could be fatal to them. This really upset me – especially not being able to see Ollie. We had spent so much time together in the weeks leading up to the birth that I was desperate for him to see Annie, to bond with her.

Jason was allowed to come, though. I was nervous before he arrived – I didn't know how he was going to react but when he walked through the big double doors, he went straight over to the incubator and stood there for ages, staring at her. His daughter.

For a split second, everything fell into place. *Yes, this is how it's meant to be,* I thought. *Now we're a proper family.*

My heart filled with love and happiness and though I knew everything about this situation was wrong, I was so overwhelmed with emotion that I touched his arm. 'It's okay,' I told him. 'I'll keep quiet. I won't tell no one.'

He looked at me then and I saw that his eyes were filled with love. He didn't speak. *It's all going to be fine*, I told myself. *I would go home with Mum when Annie got better and we'd all be together.*

Jason put his arms through the holes in the incubator to touch Annie and I didn't flinch. I wasn't angry or upset – she was his child, after all. He seemed happy, if a little overwhelmed, and for a while he didn't speak. I knew at that moment he loved our daughter too.

The social workers came while I was in Little France. I suppose I'd been expecting them but even so, when they showed up, I couldn't help bristling with indignation.

Helen and June trotted in, in their brisk little heels, full of fake smiles and concern.

'How are you doing, Tressa?' Helen asked, head cocked to one side.

'Fine,' I said guardedly. I was torn – torn between telling them how well I'd been doing and yet not wanting to talk to them at all.

I knew they held all the power over me and I resented this.

They took me down to the canteen to get a cup of tea and then, sitting opposite me, stirring their mugs, they dropped their bombshell.

'Look, Tressa, you have a big decision to make,' June started. 'Annie was registered at a Pre-birth Child Protection Case Conference as a child likely to be exposed to physical neglect and emotional abuse in the family's home environment. Therefore, as we have signalled to you previously, we have put a care plan in place to have Annie fostered.'

'What?' I spluttered. 'What do you mean? What about my aunty Marilyn?' This was my fallback plan. I knew that there was always a chance the social workers wouldn't let us go back to Mum's, so my aunty Marilyn had volunteered to take us. She was currently going through the risk assessment to foster us.

'She's fostered my cousins!' I insisted. 'We can go to her!'

June shook her head: 'No, I'm sorry, Tressa. Marilyn has failed the risk assessment because she's clinically depressed.'

'Well, what about me?' I asked. 'Aren't I going with Annie?'

'Tressa, this is where you have to make a choice,' Helen said calmly, putting her palms flat on the table in front of her. 'You can either go into care with Annie or you can return to your mother's house on your own.'

'WHAT?' I was livid! What sort of a choice was that? Of course I couldn't leave Annie. I was her mum!

'She's not going anywheres without me!' I told them vehemently. 'She's ma daughter! You're not taking her away from me. Not for a minute!'

'Well, that's your choice, Tressa...'

'That's no fucking choice at all!' I railed. 'You're taking me away from my family and everybody I know just when I need them most. Well, you can fuck off! Go on, fuck off! I don't need yous lot either!'

The other people in the canteen were staring at me now, but I didn't care. I hardly noticed their open-mouthed gawping. I was out of my mind with rage and I stood up, shaking, and screamed my head off: 'GO ON, YOU FUCKING CUNTS! FUCK OFF! LEAVE US ALONE. I'VE HAD ENOUGH OF ALL OF YOUS!'

They hurriedly gathered their files and hoisted their handbags to their shoulders, embarrassed by the attention, but I didn't care. I was a mum now and somehow that knowledge, that new and awesome responsibility, had given me a new kind of courage. Whatever happened I wouldn't let them take Annie from me. Even if it meant losing everybody I loved.

That night I cried into my pillow. I had really hoped they would let me stay with Mum – they'd told me that if things changed there was a chance but now, in the stillness of the night, I admitted to myself that Mum hadn't changed. Nothing had changed. Still, it riled me that they had failed Marilyn for being chronically depressed. It hadn't stopped her raising her own three kids

Whatever happened now, I would be on my own and I would have to try my hardest to do without my family. It broke my heart knowing that I wouldn't be able to live with Ollie again. How would he cope without me? I worried that he wouldn't get the care and attention he needed, and he would miss me. Worse, he might think I had abandoned him. He was like my own son and it tore me up inside to know I would be parted from him. None of us realised it at the time, but there would be further shocks to come.

It took three weeks before Annie was well enough to be transferred back to St John's hospital in Livingston and by then I had got used to holding her and giving her the bottle. I'd wanted to breastfeed at first but I felt too embarrassed about getting it wrong. It was hard enough to cope with the nurses' constant watchfulness whenever I was with Annie. I knew it would be too hard to do it with everyone watching me, just waiting for me to get it wrong.

As the days passed, Annie got stronger and stronger. Finally, she was well enough to come out of the intensive care unit and into a normal cot. They put her in a big double room with me so I could look after her all the time. I preferred it like this – I didn't like going out onto the ward. There, people would stare at me. They knew who I was – they whispered it behind their hands but loud enough for me to hear: 'That's the lassie from the papers.'

Then they'd turn away, pretending not to look, but I felt an itchy discomfort whenever I was on the main ward, so I tried to stay in my room with Annie as much as possible. I loved it this way – just me and her alone together. The funny thing was: she was the spitting image of Jason. Even my mum commented on it.

'She's got the same eyes as Jay, you know,' she said one day when she came to visit.

'Oh aye?' I said, nonchalantly.

'Aye, she looks just like him.'

I said nothing. She didn't know the real reason for this.

After a while, she said, 'You know, maybe it's for the best.' I knew what she was talking about.

'I mean, we've only got the three bedrooms,' she went on. 'Can you imagine eight of us in there?'

'Are you giving up on us then?' I said with a heavy heart. She was still my mum. I loved her.

'No, I'm going to fight for yous,' she replied quickly. 'It's just that maybe it'll help you and Annie get started in the right way. You know, once you've proved to the social workers you can look after her on your own then perhaps they'll let you both come back.'

'I painted the room,' I said quietly. 'I got it all ready for her.'

'Aye, I ken. Well, it'll be all nice for you then, won't it? When you come back.'

After five weeks in hospital, Annie was finally well enough

to come out. I'd been allowed to go round to my mum's house to collect all our stuff. I noticed that Mum hadn't spent the money from Gail on a cot or new clothes – but there were a couple of giant new teddy bears in my room. I didn't ask her about it. I didn't ask her about the money at all.

While I was home, I took the opportunity to give Ollie a great big cuddle and reassure him.

'You and baby coming back soon?' he asked, scrunching up his face with uncertainty.

'Yes, definitely!' I told him. 'I'll be back and then we'll go swimming together again, eh?'

'Okay,' he said. It was heartbreaking. I couldn't bear to leave him but I didn't have any choice.

Annie and I were put under the care of a new family – Abigail and Leon. They were nice enough people and they meant well, but from the word go, I felt awkward. I was living in a new home with complete strangers and a baby I'd just met, cut off from my whole family. It left me hurt and confused – my heart was ripped in two. I tried my best to be a good mum to Annie but I couldn't help worrying about Ollie and Kai. They all needed me!

Every Friday I was allowed contact with my mum and siblings at my aunty Marilyn's house. It was lovely to see them all – Annie would come too so they could all spend time with her. Then either June or Helen would pick Annie up and I'd be allowed to stay at my mum's place for the weekend. It was a difficult situation. Mum wasn't drinking as much but still, I worried for my wee brothers. On Friday and Saturday nights, I would go out with my friends and it was such a relief to be freed of all the responsibility that I ended up getting drunk and smoking hash. Mum didn't mind. I smoked and drank with her plenty of times.

The trouble was that after I got back on Sunday nights, Abigail found it hard to let me take over Annie's care again. She liked to insist on doing everything herself.

'Go on, you look exhausted,' she said. 'Don't worry – I'll bath the baby tonight.'

'No, I should do it,' I'd tell her.

'Och, no!' she insisted. 'Go on and lie down. I'll do it.'

I didn't want her doing everything for me. I thought it would end up going in her report and make it look like I wasn't taking care of Annie right. It felt like she was taking over. During the week I tried to do everything for Annie but often Abigail would interfere, taking over her feeding or her winding when I really didn't want her to. She didn't ask; she just took her off me. It got so bad that I ended up spending a lot of time in my room with Annie just so she would leave us alone.

It got harder and harder to cope. I never wanted to leave my brothers at the end of the weekend, but at the same time I knew I had to get back for Annie. I spent all week worrying about the boys and phoned my mum constantly, checking up on her, making sure she was feeding them and taking care of them right.

'Don't bloody worry,' Mum snapped one time. 'They're fine. They're fine.'

But I knew my mum's version of 'fine' didn't always tally with the truth so I'd insist she put Ollie on the phone. I wasn't satisfied until I'd spoken to him myself – checking he'd been to nursery that day, making sure he'd eaten a good tea.

One Friday I went for a contact visit at my aunty Marilyn's

and found my mum wasn't well. She was lying on my aunty's bed, in agony, not breathing right.

'I'm calling an ambulance,' I told her firmly.

'Don't be so bloody stupid,' she wheezed from the bed. But I wasn't taking no for any answer – her breathing was all weird and it was freaking me out. Once the social worker had picked up Annie, I called the ambulance. The paramedics did a quick examination and confirmed that she had pneumonia. They gave her morphine to ease her pain and then took her to the hospital.

'It's good you called when you did,' one of them said to me. 'She needs to be in hospital.'

I went back to my mum's place that weekend and spent the rest of the time getting drunk. If I hadn't been there to call an ambulance, Mum might not have made it. I wondered if the social workers ever considered how much my mum needed me when they separated us. It was all too much.

One weekend I came back to Abigail and Leon's house earlier than planned and found that they weren't in. I called up my social worker in a panic.

'Where are they?' I demanded, my stomach full of butterflies.

'Don't worry, Tressa,' the social worker replied casually. 'They've just gone up to Seton Sands.'

Abigail and Leon had a caravan up in Seton Sands and they liked to go there for the weekend sometimes.

'But they never asked ma permission if they could take Annie,' I objected. 'What right have they to take my baby away without telling me?'

'It makes no difference if they are caring for her in the

house or in the caravan,' she said, as if talking to a child. 'While they are the primary carers, they are free to care for her in either place.'

'IT MATTERS TO ME!' I screamed down the phone. 'She's my child, not theirs! They need to ask me!'

I was fuming but I had no choice. I went back to my mum's place to wait until they got back on Sunday. By now, Jason, Alex and several others had gathered at Mum's place. Everyone was drinking and smoking hash. I knew I needed to calm down so I got drunk that night too. I just couldn't understand how they could take my child away without asking. The alcohol seeped into my joints and instantly relaxed my muscles – it helped to release all the tension, to make all my worries go away. I got so drunk that night that I didn't turn up at Abigail's till the Monday morning.

The social workers told me I had to stop doing this and I knew it wasn't right but I was stressed.

'I don't know how I'm supposed to act,' I tried to explain to Helen one day. 'I love Ollie and Kai – I've known them both longer – and yet I'm supposed to forget about them all the week while I live with these strangers? It's impossible! My brothers need me.'

'Aye, but Annie needs you more, Tressa. You're her mother.'

'I feel like I'm *their* mother as well.'

'Well, that's not right, is it, Tressa?'

'I guess not – but it's true. So what if it's not right? I can't help it, can I? They're not my children but this is what the situation is and I can't change it. I can't change any of it but I'm doing my best. It just feels like it's all too much.'

It all came to a head one Friday when I was at my aunty

Marilyn's for contact. Helen was there and I was trying to tell her about Abigail taking over, how it was making it hard for me to bond with Annie. It was like they didn't take me seriously and I got so upset that I ended up having a panic attack and passing out at the bottom of the garden. When I came to, the social worker had taken Annie back to the foster carer's. I spent the following week at my mum's place. Then we had a meeting with Helen at Abigail's house.

Abigail sat and listened politely as Helen outlined my complaint against her, then she said: 'I'm sorry you feel that way, Tressa.'

It was one of the sentences that didn't mean anything – it wasn't an apology; it was just another way of saying that I was wrong.

'Why don't you come back?' she went on. 'If you come back I promise to leave you alone and not offer help unless you ask for it.'

'That's what you should have done to begin with!' I spat. I was sick of her, sick of the social workers, sick of this whole horrible situation. I felt no one took me seriously, nobody tried to help me.

Now the court case for Jason Barnes was coming up and I felt more stressed and anxious than ever before.

'I'm not coming back,' I said resolutely. 'How can you expect me to meet all my goals for my report if you try to do everything for me? It's not right.'

'Perhaps you're being a little immature,' Abigail suggested. 'Perhaps you're not thinking things through and jumping to conclusions. I'm not trying to sabotage your chances with Annie. I'm trying to help you. You can always tell me no.'

'You don't pay me any mind!' I exploded. 'I mean, how can you take my daughter away without even telling or asking me? How would you feel if someone took your daughter away without telling you?'

'It wasn't far and you knew she was in my care so I don't know why you were worried.' She was trying to smooth things over but I couldn't accept it.

'That's not the point,' I snapped. 'You should have asked. You crossed a line and I don't trust you anymore.'

There was a silence then as I looked down at Annie in her bouncy chair. Then I looked up and glowered at both Abigail and Helen.

'So you're not willing to give this placement another try?' Helen asked me.

'Nope. No way.'

And that was that. I was moved temporarily into Uphill Young People's Centre in Blairgowrie while they found a new foster carer. Fortunately, Helen thought to approach Barbara Foxton, my old foster carer, who agreed to come out of retirement to take Annie and me. It felt like the perfect solution. I knew Barbara and knew she wouldn't try to take over with the baby. But in the meantime, she needed time to get the new house ready so Annie stayed with Abigail while I was in the secure unit. It was enraging but there was nothing I could do until Barbara was ready for us.

I was up at my mum's a lot during this time and in the middle of September that year we were hit with the worst news possible. At a children's hearing it was decided that Ollie and Kai were in danger of being neglected and they were taken off my mum. That broke her heart – I knew that those boys meant everything to her. I'd done everything humanly possible to prevent it, to the point of ripping myself in two. I'd risked having my own child taken away in order to look after my little brothers, to stop them being taken into care. I'd kept my older brother's dirty little secret just so that they could stay with my mum. And yet it had happened anyway. But the social workers explained that after I fell pregnant at eleven, it was almost inevitable the others would get taken away.

So that was how it was. I blamed myself. Of course I did.

CHAPTER 13

A Fractured Life

Rain. I smiled to myself. I liked it when it rained. Everyone thought I was crazy but I honestly preferred it when the sky was grey and there was a light spatter of water on the pavements. The sun bothered me – it was always too bright, and I got hot and sticky very quickly. No, give me a driving shower or a grey, foggy morning any day over a sweltering hot summer's day. As I walked to college, I let the faint drizzle dampen my face and my clothes, pleased to feel the coolness on my skin. Now Mum had lost her boys and I had moved into Barbara's without Annie. It felt at times like my life was being run by social services. They had put a care plan in place for me to see Annie twice a week, to be increased every few weeks until Barbara's house was ready for Annie to move in. I had assumed at first that Annie would come to live with me at Barbara's soon after I moved in. But the days turned into weeks, which turned into months.

Every weekend I would go and see my mum, who was now drinking more than ever. Without the boys, she was a mess, taking kit all the time and not looking after herself. I worried about her constantly – she failed to turn up to contact meetings with the boys and this made me mad. How did she expect to get them back again if she refused to cooperate with social services?

'They're all bastards,' she railed at me one weekend, out of her mind on drink. 'They just want to treat me like a dog – scolding and rewarding me with little treats. I've had enough!'

'Dinnae say that, Mum!' I urged. 'It's not going to be forever. But if you don't see them, how do the social workers know you care?'

'I'll tell the bloody papers,' Mum went on, ignoring me. 'I've told them – if they don't give the kids back to me, I'll get Gail to do a story on them!'

This is the way my mother now behaved – if she didn't get her own way, she just went running to Gail. But not even Gail could influence social services – it was all up to my mum. She didn't seem capable of understanding this so I changed the subject.

'Have you eaten today?' I asked. She looked thin as a rake and hollow-cheeked. Her eyes were sunk deep into their sockets and she had a grey, sickly pallor, as if she hadn't been outside in months.

'Aye, I'm fine. I'm fine,' she said, lighting another roll-up from the dying one in her fingers. 'Here, have you got any money?'

'I've got my £12 pocket money,' I told her. Mum coughed into the back of her hand. A wheezy, rattling cough.

'Well, give it here, would you?' she said. 'I need it.'

So I gave it to her. It seemed she needed it more than me. By then, whenever I saw her, I felt frightened. Some part of me was always fearful about my mum and her health – her asthma was worse than ever and she didn't look after herself. I left that day wondering, not for the first time, if I would ever see her again. Social services told me I worried too much about her, that I sometimes failed to prioritise my own needs above hers. But it was hard – I had always looked out for my mum, protected her. I couldn't just turn that feeling off overnight. Also, I felt responsible now for her declining health – it was because of me that Ollie and Kai got taken away. If she fell to pieces now, I couldn't live with myself. So I tried my hardest to look after her as best I could.

Back at Barbara's, things were going well. I was happy living there and my contact meetings with Annie were always the highlight of my week. When she was brought in to see me, her face lit up with delight and she called out: 'Mama!' My heart just melted. She was growing up so fast! I played with her, sang songs and made up silly games – I could spend hours and hours with her, and it felt like no time had passed at all. She was my world – my everything. I looked in her face and saw such open, innocent love; it killed me to have to say goodbye every time she returned to Abigail's place.

'When is she coming to live with me?' I asked Helen at our next meeting.

'Soon, soon,' she smiled, hardly looking up from her file where she was ticking boxes in a long form.

'You say that every time!' I fumed. 'I'm her mother. She should be with me.'

'Look, we just need to make sure that Barbara's place is all fixed up well for Annie – she's a toddler now and safety is key.'

'Aye, but how long does it take to put up a baby gate?' I grumbled.

'Tressa, don't worry,' she soothed. 'You've made excellent progress in your care of Annie. We can all see that. You two have got a really lovely bond.'

I knew that. I didn't have to be told – I loved Annie so much. She was such a happy, adorable little girl and as she got more mobile and started moving about, I loved sitting down on the floor playing with her.

I was going to Deans Community High School during the week and I settled in well with my classes. Finally, after six months, Annie came to live with me permanently. She had her own room next to mine and every morning I'd take Annie to the crèche while I did my lessons. Then, in the afternoon, Barbara would pick her up and I'd meet them both after school at home. It was wonderful to have Annie back with me full-time and I was grateful to Barbara for having us. I tried to prove to everyone that I could do this – I could be a good mum and keep up with my schoolwork.

For Annie's first birthday we had a big party at the local soft play centre, Spacebugs, and though my Mum wasn't there, Ollie and Kai came along with their foster carers. Seeing them was so bittersweet – I missed Ollie so much. He still came to me for big hugs but he was definitely becoming more distant. Without being able to spend time with him, I knew he was forgetting me. But I tried to put this out of my mind, as it was just so lovely to have all the kids together in the same place. I was given £50 to spend on a birthday present for Annie so

I bought her a pink trike that she pedalled around the place, squealing with delight and amazement.

She was growing into such a lovely little girl – gorgeous blonde hair and big blue eyes. I loved every single part of her. I would twirl her soft hair into bunches and spent ages picking out her outfit every day. For this occasion I'd dressed her in a sweet blue corduroy dress with a white top underneath. She looked adorable and I was so proud of her. At the party she tried to climb all over the soft play equipment but she was only just beginning to pull herself up.

'Come on,' I encouraged, sitting next to her on the brightly coloured plastic mats, and she crawled towards me. Then she held onto my legs and arms as she tried to pull herself up. I giggled as she set about this task, with a look of serious concentration on her face.

'Look at you!' I exclaimed, clapping my hands in delight. 'Aren't you a clever girl! Up on your feet like that!'

She turned round and gave me a mesmerising smile. It made me want to just eat her up! It was only a matter of weeks before she was on her feet for real and zipping around the place, making full use of the newly found freedom.

I felt my confidence as a mother grow every day. Still, it didn't take much to knock me off course. Once, after a hard day at school, I summoned up the last of my energy to feed and bathe her. Then I changed her into her lemon sleepsuit – the one with the rabbits on – and cooed to her softly as I took her up to her room. I gave her her milk as usual and then I put her in her cot and tried to settle her to sleep.

But the moment I turned my back, she started screaming.

'Oh come on now, poppet,' I walked back towards her and

picked her up again. 'You've got to sleep now. For Mummy. Please, lie down now and go to sleep. It's sleep time.'

I gave her another cuddle and put her back in her cot. She looked at me with big eyes and I smiled at her. Then, when I saw her eyelids start to droop and close, I tiptoed carefully out of the room. But I hadn't got two feet away before she started screaming again. I sighed and went back to the cot.

At that moment, Barbara popped her head round the door.

'You've got to leave her, hen,' she whispered.

'But she's crying,' I replied, biting down hard on my thumbnail.

'Aye, she's crying for attention and she knows that it works because you're giving in to her,' she explained through a thin smile. 'You've got to let her cry – she'll never learn if you pick her up every time. Come on.'

So I had no choice but to follow her out.

I sat downstairs for the next twenty minutes, biting my nails and grinding my teeth as I listened to the screams of my daughter through the ceiling.

'Don't give in,' warned Barbara, who was chopping vegetables on the counter by the oven.

'But maybe she's come out of her sleep bag,' I fretted. 'What if she's got something wrong with her?'

'Look, Tressa, we've been over this,' Barbara sighed, putting down her knife and pursing her lips. 'There's absolutely nothing wrong with her. If you go to her now, it'll be ten times worse tomorrow night and the night after. She has to self-settle. It's part of the process.'

I held out as long as I could, I really did, but after forty-five minutes of incessant screaming, punctuated with heart-wrenching cries of 'Mummy!', I couldn't take it any longer.

Her crying went right through me – I couldn't concentrate on anything and the more I tried to ignore her, the more upset I got. I was beside myself with worry and, eventually, I leapt out of the chair and raced upstairs.

'Tressa!' Barbara called out after me but I didn't pay her any notice. This was my baby! My daughter! And I was responsible for her. What if she was teething? What if she was in pain? It wasn't fair to let her cry like that. Poor thing had been through enough changes in her life already – maybe she just needed a cuddle from her mum.

I knew it would go into Barbara's reports to social services, and perhaps Barbara was trying to do the right thing by me, trying to help me, but it felt like everything I did was scrutinised. I was trying to do everything right but I couldn't go against my deepest instincts. It made me feel like I had to prove myself all the time. It was hard enough being a mum at thirteen but everything was made harder still by the fact that I was being watched constantly. In the evenings, with the eyes of the whole family on me, I felt that my every move was being judged, assessed. It made me nervous, knowing that every detail would go into the reports. So after a few months, I started to take Annie to my room to play with her in the evenings. Together, when it was just the two of us, it was easier to relax and enjoy being with her.

There were other tensions, too. Most of the time, I was in every night with Annie, but one time I was allowed out with my friends from High School. We had a great time and it was a relief to be a kid again for a while – but I lost track of time and when I came in late at 10.30pm, Barbara was very cross with me.

The next day she sat me down.

'I know you're finding it hard to cope with Annie,' she started.

'Wait, what do you mean?' I was confused. I thought everything was fine.

'Well, I can see that you enjoy being out with your friends. Perhaps you want to think about whether it might be best for Annie if you looked at finding her a more permanent placement with someone?'

'What do you mean?' I said again. I felt my whole body tense up. I didn't like where this was going.

'I mean it might be best for her to look at going down the adoption route,' Barbara said carefully. 'You have got your whole life ahead of you, Tressa. You can be a mother again someday but perhaps it isn't right for you now? Annie could have a fresh start. Eh? Something to think about anyway.'

My heart sank – I felt like crying right there but I didn't let my emotions show. I couldn't let her see how much her words had hurt me. I just gave the briefest of nods and went upstairs to my room. If Barbara didn't have faith in me, what chance did I have? It felt like the whole system was against me.

'You better bloody not!' Mum screeched when I reported this conversation over the phone the next day. 'That's my grandchild you've got there.'

'I don't want to,' I told her earnestly. 'I'm just, well… I'm just disappointed. I thought everything was going okay. I thought she believed in me.'

'I'll bloody kill myself if you give that baby away,' Mum went on, barely acknowledging my words, turning the whole thing back to herself. As usual.

'Oh Jesus!' I exploded. 'Forget it, okay? Just forget I ever said anything.' I knew better than to look to my mother for sympathy and support. I couldn't win. Whichever way I turned, I couldn't win.

I tried to keep my head up, to keep going, but now I was getting abuse from some of the kids on the way to school. The name-calling was bad enough – shouts of 'slut' would echo in my ears all the way to the school gate – but a couple of times I got stuff chucked at me and that was horrible. I complained to the school and they agreed that I could come in at 9.30am from then on, after all the other kids had gone in.

But it became harder and harder just to leave the house each morning. The one time I tried to take Annie swimming at the local pool, we got turned away.

'Sorry,' said the bored-looking teenager behind the desk, picking at her flaking nail polish. 'Under-fives need to be accompanied by someone over sixteen.'

'But I'm her mum!' I was outraged.

'It doesn't matter,' the girl said, popping chewing gum in her mouth. 'If you're under the age of sixteen, you can't be responsible for a child under five.'

'I've been coming here for ages,' I spluttered. 'I used to bring ma wee brother here when he was three!'

'Aye, but you were pregnant then,' the girl said with a nasty smile. 'We thought you were older.'

I was trying my hardest, I really was, but now Mum's health was really bad and every time I went there, I got sucked into her world and her problems. There was always a drama kicking off at her place and she was drinking so much by then that I couldn't remember the last time I'd seen her without a can in her hand. My head was a mess and I felt like a failure. Nobody believed in me; nobody had faith in me. One night, I was listening to the Leona Lewis song 'Bleeding Love' on my CD player and the feelings just took over me. I started to sob. I couldn't take it any more. My life felt like it wasn't my own and I didn't know how to keep everybody happy. If I tried to help my mum, Barbara and the social workers complained, and if I didn't help her, she went into free fall. She was still my mother and I cared about her so much. I wanted to be a good mum, too, but the pressure on me was immense. Suddenly, something occurred to me. I wandered through to the bathroom and found a razor. I took it to my room and broke it out of its plastic case. It was so thin – so sharp and thin. I turned it over in my hand, marvelling at how light it was. Then I held it to my forearm and pressed down hard.

The pain was sharp and intense, and it made me catch my breath – but it was also the best feeling I'd had all day. The bright red blood appeared immediately and started to drip down onto my bed sheet, but I hardly noticed. I held the razor against another place in my arm and slashed at it again. And again. And again.

A wave of relief flooded through me – I watched as the blood dribbled down onto my covers and made crimson smears on my sheets. Then I looked at my arm, at the gashes I'd just made, and with my thumb and forefinger, I tried to pull each wound apart to increase the pain and summon up the sharp release that freed me from my worries and my fears. Afterwards, I felt light and happy; I slept better that night than I had in weeks.

The next morning Barbara took one look at the scabby red lines on my arm and asked me what I'd done. I told her. I didn't see the point of hiding it – she'd find out eventually. Of course, it went straight into the reports but by that point I didn't care. I couldn't please everyone. I couldn't even try – they had their agenda and they were just waiting for me to slip up. Just a few weeks later it all came to a head, and Barbara and I had a massive falling out.

'I don't want to live here anymore,' I shouted at her. 'You don't think I can be a good mum to Annie. It feels like you're always watching me, waiting for me to do the wrong thing. I can't win!'

Barbara looked at me and sighed.

'Well, if that's your decision,' she said evenly, 'then I won't object.'

'Fine,' I said. It was sad – she hadn't even tried to persuade me to stay. She'd had enough too. 'But you tell the social worker I won't be split up again. You tell them that! I'm not going anywhere without Annie.'

'I'll see what they say,' she said quietly, folding a tea towel neatly in front of her. Then she left the room.

When I got back from school the following day, I walked in the house to find that Barbara had packed all my stuff. Large holdalls full of my clothes and belongings were lined up neatly in the hallway. Suddenly, I had butterflies in my stomach – I was being moved on again. I couldn't believe it had all fallen apart so quickly. I was a bundle of nerves. It was too much, but I couldn't change my mind now and I knew Barbara didn't want me around any longer. That much was clear!

I couldn't let her see me panicking so I held down my nerves.

When she appeared in the hallway, she looked at my bags, as if checking they were still there. I watched and waited for her to speak. I wanted her to tell me she was sorry that I was leaving, but she didn't. She didn't say a word.

So I asked her: 'Where am I going?'

'Helen says they can't find another foster placement for you both at the moment so you're going to Letham Young People's Centre,' she said formally. It was like I was already gone. There was no emotion – nothing.

Half an hour later, Helen arrived.

'Okay?' she smiled at me. 'Ready to go?'

CHAPTER 14

The Truth

After the move to Letham, things went downhill very quickly. At first, I worked hard to make sure the placement was a success. I helped to paint the large double room I shared with Annie, arranged the furniture and made the place nice. But it quickly became clear that group living didn't suit me.

Letham was a lawless place where the kids ran riot. We had many different carers coming and going, and though they tried to discipline us, they just couldn't. This was where they sent the kids they couldn't find foster homes for. Here, every kid had issues. No one went to school, and everyone took drugs and drank – and the youngest was ten years old. I hated it and I didn't want my daughter to be around any of those people.

Increasingly, I started to escape to my mum's place in order to avoid the people in Letham. I was also cutting myself a lot, as it seemed the only way I could cope with the pressure. The social workers sent me to the psychiatric unit to have my mental health assessed. I didn't see how it was meant to help. Every time, I came out in floods of tears and in a worse state than before – but I didn't have any choice. The doctors said I wasn't mentally unwell, just depressed by the circumstances in my life. Well, that made sense.

Somewhere along the way, I lost the plot. I don't know when exactly but after just a few weeks, I was at breaking point. During one visit from my social worker, she left the room briefly and I noticed that her bag was open. I went into her wallet and took three notes out then stuffed them in my back pocket. She figured out it was me almost immediately and though she gave me the opportunity to hand it back, I pretended that I didn't know what she was talking about. I don't know why I did it – I really don't – her purse was just there and in a split second I decided to take £60. She threatened to search me and it was then that I confessed and handed back the money but by then I was in a real state. I went back to my room and cut myself really badly. The police were called, and the social workers came and said they thought it would be best for me if I had some respite from Annie. So they took her away. I started screaming at them. I was mad and out of control. It was like all the tension and upheavals of the past few months exploded in one go. I'd held it together for as long as I could but now I couldn't cope and I didn't know who to turn to or what to do. I loved Annie and I wanted to be there for her but right at that moment I could barely take care of myself, let alone her.

Without Annie, my life spiralled out of control. I didn't see the point in going to school; I just wanted to go out and get drunk all the time.

Now fourteen, I felt like a failure and I took whatever I could get my hands on just to block out reality. One night in June 2008, I absconded to my mum's place again. I couldn't bear to be separated from everyone in my life, and there I felt safe and secure. I begged her not to tell the police I was there, so when they came banging on the door at around midnight, she told me to hide under her bed. Then she blatantly lied to them and told them that she didn't know where I was.

They left but Mum wasn't certain they had gone so I stayed under her bed for about half an hour, just in case they marched back in.

While I was waiting to come out of hiding, Jason arrived back home. Mum obviously told him where I was so he came up to find me, and I just saw the white flashes on his trainers as he walked into the room and sat down on the bed, where I'd left my half-drunk bottle of Buckfast.

'Here, Tress,' Jason called out, knowing full well I was lying underneath him on the floor. 'Can I have the rest of this Buckie?'

'NO!' I shouted back, edging my way out from my hiding place.

'Ha! Too late,' he laughed as I stood up next to him. 'I've already drunk it.'

I could see he was plastered and felt a twinge of irritation. I sat down on the bed next to him and he handed me the bottle so I could drain the dregs.

'Here, Tressa,' he slurred, putting his arm around me. 'I love you, you know?'

'Aye, I love you too as a brother,' I replied.

'No!' he said, holding me by the shoulders now so I was forced to look him in the face. His eyes were bloodshot and his head bobbed unsteadily. 'I *really* love you. Not as a sister.'

My heart started to thump. What was he saying?

'What? No, Jason,' I shook my head vehemently. 'No. You're with Kate. I'm your sister. It's never going to happen.'

'I can't help how I feel!' he said, holding out his hands in a gesture of helplessness. He took my hands in his then. 'Come on, let's do it one more time. One more time.'

My blood ran cold – at that moment all those painful, humiliating encounters from the past surfaced once again. I thought I'd put them all behind me. I thought I was free from all this. Why? Why did he have to start it up again? I slid backwards on the bed, away from him.

'No, get off me!' I shouted as I struggled to yank my hands from his grasp and stood up, shocked and upset. His face fell and he sat there for a moment as I stood over him, breathing hard.

Then he pushed himself up off the bed and moved towards the door.

'I'm going to tell Mum,' he slurred. 'I'm not bothered any more. I'm going to tell Mum.'

'No no! You can't do that!' and I pushed him back down on the bed. He was so drunk I could tell he meant it – he was going to tell her everything and then I'd get into big trouble. And then Mum would never get the boys back.

'MUM!' Jason yelled out. 'MUM!'

'Oh no, Jason!' I begged, crying now. 'Please don't, Jason. Please don't tell her.'

But it was too late.

'What is it?' Mum called out from downstairs.

'It's nothing, nothing!' I shouted back, panicked and scared. I tried to make my voice sound as normal as possible. 'It's nothing, just Jason.'

'Oh right, nae bother,' Mum said.

When I knew she definitely wasn't coming back up the stairs, I whispered urgently to Jason, 'You have to go to Dad's place.'

'No, I'm going to tell Mum,' he insisted, swaying on the bed.

'You're not!' I said and ran out of the room. I went to the kitchen and called my dad, begging him to take Jason for the night.

Then I called a taxi for him.

I was beside myself and so dismayed by the whole thing. For three years it had all been forgotten. Ever since that time in the brickyard – he hadn't come near me since. I had tried to forget it all, to put it out of my mind but now he was bringing it all up again and I felt that I was on the point of a complete breakdown.

I managed to keep him upstairs until the taxi arrived, and then I shoved a couple of quid into his hand and led him downstairs.

He was still shouting for my mum as he staggered unsteadily down.

'What? What's all the shouting for?' Mum was annoyed now.

'It's nothing,' I said. 'He just wants to tell you that he's going to Dad's place.'

I was nearly hysterical but I couldn't let him do this. I couldn't bear the thought of it all coming out.

But Mum wasn't stupid – she didn't buy my excuses.

'No, tell me, Jay,' she urged as he half-stumbled, half-fell out of the front door. 'Tell me!'

But I didn't give him a chance to reply – I forced him into the back of the cab and slammed the door shut. Then I ran back into the house and up the stairs. I couldn't hold back the tears any longer. I was sobbing when I called up the staff at Letham, begging them to come and collect me.

The police came within fifteen minutes and I cried all the way back to Letham. I burst in the door and went straight to my room but the staff followed quickly afterwards.

'Tressa!' shouted Neil, one of the staff at the home, through the door. 'Are you okay? Let me in!'

'No. I'm going to kill myself!' I shouted, barely knowing what I was saying anymore. I went to the bathroom but in another second he had unlocked the door with his staff key and was at my side.

I collapsed on the floor, sobbing, unable to move.

How could I tell them? How? Annie would be taken away and then I'd never see her again. But Jason was going to tell anyway. Oh, what did it matter anymore? I couldn't keep this bottled up inside any longer. It was killing me.

All this time, Neil had kept hold of me and was leading me back in the room. I could barely breathe I was crying so hard.

'Please, tell me,' he said gently. 'What's wrong? What's happened?'

'It's Jason,' I managed to say between sobs.

'Jason – your brother?'

'Aye – Annie is Jason's. My brother is my baby's dad.'

It felt so good to say it at last – to say those words I'd been so afraid of for so long. And yet here I was, going right over the edge, into an unknown world. I knew that from this moment nothing would ever be the same again.

Neil looked up at Mel, the other member of staff who had followed us into the room.

Then he asked me to repeat what I'd just said.

'My brother, Jason, is Annie's dad.'

There was a very long silence then.

'I need to go and get the other members of staff,' Neil said seriously. Then he got up and Mel came and sat next to me as I sobbed uncontrollably. Neil returned a few moments later with two other staff members.

'Tressa,' he said. 'Tressa, I'd like you to tell us what you just said to me.'

Then I looked at them all and tried to wipe away the tears with the ball of my hand. I breathed in and out, hard.

'My brother had been abusing me when I was younger,' I told them. 'And I fell pregnant and then I had a baby, and Annie is his.'

Then Neil said: 'Do you understand we're going to have to get the police? We cannae just let this go.'

'No, no, no,' I begged. 'Please don't. You don't have to tell them.'

'Aye, we do,' he said. And I knew they would. They didn't have any choice.

I was exhausted now, overcome by the events of the evening, by all the crying and the despair. Mel eased off my shoes and helped me to bed. They turned out the light as they left the room and I fell asleep straight away.

CHAPTER 15

The Fallout

BANG BANG BANG.
The heavy thump of a closed fist reverberated on my door.

'Tressa? Are you awake, love? The police are here to see you.'

Mel's voice came to me through a deep and dream-free sleep. Gradually, I stirred, turning my head on my pillow so that I was facing the window.

'What?' I yelled. 'What is it?'

'Police, Tressa. The police are here.'

I didn't think anything of it. These days I was always in trouble with the police. I ran away so much that they were often called to pick me up and take me back to Letham. Sometimes twice a night.

I pushed myself off the bed and held my throbbing forehead. My stomach lurched and I tried to keep down the bile that was now sliding up my throat. I rubbed hard at my face to wake myself but my whole body felt like it needed ten more hours of sleep. I shrugged my blue dressing gown over my pajamas, hooked my slippers onto my toes and trudged through to the lounge.

There, a man and a woman were sitting on the sofa. They both got to their feet when I came in. What was this about? Usually, the only police who came to see me were in uniform. These two were plain-clothed.

'Tressa,' Mel smiled at me and then nodded towards the officers. 'The police are here to take a statement.'

'We're here because of the things you told the staff last night,' the woman said.

My stomach plunged towards the floor. It hit me all at once. I'd told them! I'd told them about Jason last night and in a second I was wide awake.

'I don't want to press charges,' I said quickly. I regretted opening my big mouth. Why had I been so stupid? In that instant I knew that I'd never get Annie back.

'You don't have to press charges,' the officer said. 'Please, sit down.'

I sunk back onto the sofa in a daze.

'We'll do a DNA test to prove paternity. If it turns out that Jason is the father and a crime has been committed then that is a criminal matter.'

I was devastated. Right then, I realised the consequences of what I'd done. Jason would hate me for this – they all would. They'd turn against me – the only people I had left in my life: my mum, my brothers, my aunties, my sister... Everyone! They'd disown me. Everyone loved Jason. Mum always took his side. I was going to split the family up for good and no one would ever forgive me. What about the papers? Oh my God! What would happen when the papers found out? It was only a matter of time. And then everyone would say Mum was a bad mother. I shook my head from side to side, trying to block out the inevitable. I'd have to tell them now. I didn't have any choice.

So for the next hour and a half, I talked to the police about the abuse, about what Jason had done to me since I was seven years old. I didn't go into all the details – it was too hard, too painful – but they asked lots of questions and I did my best to answer them. The lady police officer seemed really nice; she was kind and gentle. The man barely said anything – just kept his head bowed as he scribbled down everything I said.

I couldn't answer all her questions. Some things were hazy – the times when Jason gave me hash and then touched me, I had no idea what had happened or how long it had gone on for. But I told them about all the main occasions. And I said I knew Annie was Jason's because of the time he took me to the brickyard. The whole way through my pregnancy, doctors had questioned the dates, saying that they didn't quite add up. Now I could explain why – it wasn't Jason Barnes's baby after all.

'Okay.' The woman turned to her colleague with one eyebrow raised and he nodded solemnly. 'Okay, Tressa. That should do for now. Thank you for talking to us today. I know this hasn't been easy. We'll be in touch when we have news.'

They got up and Mel showed them out. I just sat there, feeling light as a feather. The pressure that had been weighing down on me all this time was suddenly gone. I could have floated away at that minute. I didn't have to keep the secret any longer. But almost a second later, a new and more terrifying thought entered my mind: my family! They would all hate me. I was going to lose everybody and there was nothing I could do about it.

The following month passed by in a haze of drink and drugs. I tried to put it all to the back of my mind but as I suspected, Jason denied everything and my family refused to believe me. My mum said she wasn't going to take sides but at the same time she never said once that she believed me. I tried to block it all out. I didn't want to think about it. I knew my carers were worried for me, and every time I escaped from the unit, they contacted the police to pick me up. I just wanted to be left alone – I was sick of everyone and everything in my life. I'd screwed everything up and I felt it would just be better for everyone if I disappeared.

The DNA came back as a positive match for Jason and on 29 July 2008 he was charged with statutory rape and incest. I was pleased. Finally, I thought, finally they would believe me!

'I'm not taking sides,' was all Mum would say to me on the phone that night.

'What do you mean you're not taking sides?' I was distraught. She was my mum – my daughter was my brother's baby. He had been sixteen and I was eleven at the time of conception. How could she not take sides?

'Just what I said,' she reiterated. 'You're both ma children and I can't take sides. I'll support you both.'

'How is that supporting me?' I screamed down the phone. 'How is that not taking sides?'

I slammed the phone down, shaking with indignation. After all that, after all the years I'd kept quiet to protect her! And now, when she was faced with the truth, she still refused to support me.

I climbed out of my window in the unit that night and went out drinking with some of my pals. We bought hash and I got absolutely off my head. The police picked me up at 1am and took me back. But I ran away again.

The next evening at 8pm I returned to the unit.

'Can I call my mum?' I asked the staff. They gave me the phone.

'Mum?' I said when she picked up the phone.

'What are you doing calling me?' she spat. I was shocked at her anger.

'What's up?' I said.

'I'll tell you what's up. I've got your brother Jason here and he tried to kill himself last night!'

'Oh Christ!'

'All because of YOU!' she screeched. She was shouting so loud now that I had to hold the phone away from my ear.

'What did you have to go throwing around accusations like that for, you lying bastard!'

'I'm not lying!' I screamed back. 'I'm telling the truth. The DNA proves it!'

'Aye, you're lying! You wee boot!'

'Tell her to fuck off!' I could hear Jason shouting in the background. 'I'm going to fucking kill her! That girl should be six feet under!'

'Shut up!' I yelled back. 'Shut up – you're nothing but a bloody paedophile. I hate you both and wish you were dead!'

'You're drunk,' Mum yelled. 'You're drunk and you're a lying bastard. Go away and go to sleep.'

I slammed down the phone, shaking, and ran into the bathroom. After all these years of hiding the truth and protecting my mum, this was the ultimate betrayal.

I'd always been in the wrong, I realised then. I could never do anything right in her eyes. It was always about her wonderful son. I'd never get her love, no matter what. And as this was going through my mind, I eased the cord from my tracksuit bottoms out of the waistband and climbed onto the toilet seat.

The staff were banging at the door but I didn't open it.

No... it would be better for everyone if I just disappeared. I tied one end of the cord to the light fitting, taking care to do a double knot. I gave it a good yank to make sure it was solid. Then I tied the other end of the cord around my neck.

The last thing that went through my mind before I jumped was: *I'll never see my baby again...*

I woke up in St John's hospital and once I realised what I'd done and that it hadn't worked, the tears just refused to stop. I felt so stupid and embarrassed that I hadn't succeeded. I wanted to die. More than anything in the world I just wanted to die. I had nothing left to live for – just more pain and misery ahead. My daughter was never coming back. My family all hated me and I didn't see the point of making the pain go on any longer. They couldn't be angry at a corpse. If I died, it would make everything go away – they could just get on with their lives and forget all about it.

The nurses were kind enough but I was so unhappy, I didn't

really care anymore what happened to me. Eventually, one of them said there was a phone call for me. I got out of bed and went to the nurse's station to pick up the call.

'It's me,' my mum's voice came down the line.

'What?' I asked dully, no longer angry or upset. Just tired. Tired of everything.

'I… I just wanted to say I'm sorry,' Mum said. 'I love you. I love both of you and this is really difficult. I'm not saying I don't believe you – I'm just not saying anything. Okay?'

'Yeah, whatever,' I sighed and replaced the phone in the cradle.

Doctors came and went, days and nights melted together – it was all the same. Nothing mattered to me anymore.

The psychiatrist came to see me again.

'I just wish they hadn't found me in time,' I told her honestly. 'I want to die.'

'Is there nothing you feel it's worth living for? Your child? Your sister?'

'Aye, I wouldn't mind seeing them both one last time but, you know, they're never coming back to me so what's the point?'

The services all talked to each other behind my back; I just lay on my side in St John's hospital, praying for death. The moment I got out, I could try again. And this time I'd get it right. Angry calls kept coming from all members of the family – even Dionne turned against me. She said that since Jason's arrest, neither she nor Ollie or Kai was allowed to see him. Since he was living at my mum's, she wasn't even allowed to go home anymore. Her family has been taken away from her and it was all my fault. I agreed with her – I didn't even try to argue. I just said sorry and hung up. What else was there to say? I blamed myself. If I hadn't got drunk and gone to my mum's that night, I would never have said anything. It would have been better that way.

After my revelation, the social workers told me it would be better if Annie was put up for adoption. I knew that would happen. They also told me that the psychiatric report came back saying that I was at high risk of further suicide attempts. I laughed bitterly to myself. I loved the way they repeated things I'd already told them!

It all went over my head. I didn't care. I didn't care. I didn't care. They could do what they liked to me. In the end, I would kill myself.

It was the one decision left to me and they weren't going to take it away that easily.

CHAPTER 16

Lock-Up

'Oh God, what have you done?' I breathed as I saw the police car pull up outside Letham. I knew it was for me – and I had a terrible feeling I knew why. When I was released from hospital, I was sent straight back to Letham but, once again, I did everything I could to escape.

'I'm sorry,' Mel said, urgency in her voice. 'It was the only way. We can't keep you safe here, Tressa.'

So that's why Mel had been acting funny all morning. I'd been trying to get out but every time I went to leave, she kept finding little jobs for me. First it was to help her sort the post, then she asked me to help her get the channels right on the TV and then it was the washing up. I kept telling her I wanted to go but every time I pulled on my jacket, she directed me towards a new job. Now I knew she had been trying to keep me here for a reason.

'Oh no you don't!' I shouted and then bolted out of the

front door. The policemen were just getting out of the car when I came flying out of the unit. The taller one broke into a run – his legs were so long, I hadn't got far down the road when he caught up with me, grabbing me by the shoulders so my legs swung out from under me.

I tried desperately to shake him off, bending down, writhing one way and then the next, shrugging off my jacket so he just had hold of my clothes. But he took me by the wrists. I knew this policeman – he'd picked me up loads of times before. He was actually quite nice to me but right at that moment I could have killed him.

'Get off! Get the fuck off me!' I screamed.

'Tressa!' he said. 'Calm down. Just calm down! Please! I can't let you go.'

At that minute I saw Helen come running up the road to meet us, her ponytail bobbing behind her head. She'd obviously been in the police car too.

'Tressa!'

'What are yous here for?' I yelled, now frightened.

'We're here to take you to St Katherine's,' she said, one hand on her hip, breathless from running.

'No! Don't make me go there, Helen!' I begged. 'Please. I won't do nothing. I won't try and run away or do anything stupid.'

'I'm sorry,' Helen said, with one hand on my shoulder. 'We have to. There was an Emergency Hearing after your suicide attempt. There is now a Section 69 warrant on you, which means we are putting you in a secure unit for your own safety. Tressa, your behavior is putting yourself and others at risk. I'm sorry – it's the only way.'

I stopped squirming and just looked at her. This was what I had been dreading. I knew about St Katherine's; it was a secure unit for kids – basically a children's prison. You couldn't go out at all. You couldn't even see your friends or family. I'd heard there were some really bad kids in there too – murderers even! I started to shake. I didn't want to admit it but I was terrified. I yanked my jacket out of the policeman's hands and pulled it back on.

'Do you want to pack?' Helen asked. 'Or would you like me to do it?'

'I'll fucking do it,' I spat and then walked back into the unit.

My heart was going at a million beats a minute as I sat in the back of the police car on the way to St Katherine's. My nails were already bitten down to pathetic little stubs but still I chewed on my scabbed fingers, unable to fully understand what was happening to me.

What WAS happening to me?

What had I done? What had I done?

I gripped my rucksack tight against my chest as I tried to imagine what was in store. *I'll get stabbed in there! They'll fucking murder me! This is wrong. This is all wrong.*

Helen sat next to me the whole way and explained that it wouldn't be too bad, that it was for my own good. She kept going on and on about how Letham couldn't keep me safe anymore. The absconding, the suicide attempts – I needed secure accommodation, as I was in extreme danger.

'I just got a fright,' I told her. 'That's all – I don't need to be in St Katherine's. I haven't done anything wrong! Please, Helen, please don't make me go.'

But she wouldn't hear any of it. The car wound its way through the backstreets of Edinburgh while I tried to keep the panic at bay.

It took about twenty minutes and when we pulled up at a grey terraced block, the tall policeman got out and opened up my door.

'Come on, Tressa. Let's go.'

I didn't have any choice. I got out of the car, taking my rucksack, while the policeman retrieved my big suitcase from the boot.

Helen stayed inside the car, leaning over in the seat to talk to me.

'I'll be coming to see you soon, okay?' she said, a brief smile flickering over her soft features. 'Trust me, Tressa. This is for the best.'

I was so nervous now that my hands were shaking.

'Can I just have a wee smoke before I go inside?' I asked.

She nodded and the policeman sighed, putting the case down on the pavement.

My hands were shaking so much I could barely get the fag out of the packet. I sucked in hard, trying to take in as much nicotine as possible into my lungs. There was no smoking in St Katherine's. No smoking! How was I going to survive?

I smoked the fag all the way to the stub – then I lit another from the end and smoked that too. Then another. The policeman was sighing now and rolling his eyes but Helen said it was okay so I chain-smoked three fags in a row. I was about to light my fourth when she said, 'Okay, Tressa. That's enough!'

'One more, please! Just one more!' I wanted to delay the moment I had to go in for as long as possible.

'It's not going to be that bad,' she said. 'Really! I'm going to come and see you every three weeks. Now come on – in you go.'

There were three of them waiting for me when we rang the bell – two men and a woman. After the policeman told them my name, he turned around and went back to the car. I wanted to run out after him but with three of them blocking my way, I knew I had no choice.

My bags were taken into one room – to be searched – and I was led into another room by a small, bouncy lady with curly brown hair.

'We have to search you, Tressa,' she said. 'Please take off your clothes and put them on this chair. You can leave your underwear on.'

It was humiliating. I pulled off my jeans and shirt, and then the lady made me turn around so she could check I wasn't hiding anything in my knickers. She checked over all the clothes and then instructed me to lift up my arms.

'Okay, now I've got to check the bra, so don't be alarmed,' she said.

She reached out towards me and lifted the underneath of my bra away from my chest, just to see if there was anything concealed there. It was horrible.

After I was allowed to dress again, I was shown into my room. It was tiny, with disgusting lime-green walls. There was a brick bed along one wall with a mattress about an inch thick, covered by a thin blanket. Above that there was a small, uncovered pillow. In the corner there was a toilet. A white plastic unit was screwed into the wall but it had nothing on it – no drawers, no TV, no hangers for clothes. Right up high on the wall was a small window – no curtains – with plastic squares, like little bars. This really did feel like prison. I bit down hard on my lip – I didn't want her to see me cry.

'Get settled in, Tressa,' said the woman who had searched me. 'We'll come back and check on you in a bit.'

'What about my stuff? My pillow case?'

'You won't have one for now,' she replied. 'Not until you've settled in and we know what you are like. We need to know that you're not going to use it in the wrong way.'

Then she closed the big metal door behind her and I heard the lock clank shut.

I looked around me and in that moment, I lost it. I was fourteen and I was in jail. I broke down, crying. I sat down on the brick bed and held my face in my hands. How had it come to this? Why was I being locked up? Everything was such a mess. I wondered if I'd ever see my daughter again. I let myself fall sideways onto the bed and felt the waves of sadness come crashing over me, over and over again. Did my mum know I was here? Did she even care? I used the loo paper to dab at my wet cheeks.

I lost track of time but a while later I heard the lock turn again and the woman came back in carrying a tray of food. She was like my personal prison guard! I'd seen her face a few times at the long thin window at my door, checking up on me. They had nothing to worry about – there was nothing in here I could hurt myself with. They'd already taken away the cord of my zipper top and my shoelaces, plus I hadn't been given any of my clothes or belongings yet so the room was practically empty. I had no idea what she meant by settling in! How was I supposed to settle without my stuff?

'Here,' she said, placing the tray on the white unit. 'Have some lunch. You look like you need it.'

I lay on the mattress, curled up into a ball, and I rolled onto my other side so I faced the wall. I didn't want any of her food! The door closed and the lock went again. The lock! Why was I being locked up like a bloody criminal?

Anger flooded my body, and I shot up and stared at the tray – it looked disgustingly healthy! Steamed vegetables, chicken and rice, all on a paper plate with a plastic fork. There was no knife. I picked up the tray and hurled it at the door.

'I don't want your shitty lunch!' I screamed as the food spattered over the door and onto the floor. A few small white grains of rice stuck to the window in the door, which made me feel weirdly happy for a split second. Now, whenever she did her checks, she could look at the rice!

Dinner was delivered to my cell a few hours later by the same lady as before. She tutted and shook her head when she saw the mess I'd made of my last meal, but she made no attempt to clear it up. She just stepped over it and put my new tray down in the same place as before, on the white plastic unit.

I noticed that she kept her keycard on a belt loop on her trousers and wore small diamond stud earrings and no make-up. She looked kind, but stern.

'Where's my stuff?' I asked her sullenly. She tilted her head to one side, as if expecting me to say something else.

'I beg your pardon?' she said. I knew what she was after and, exasperated, I repeated my question: 'Can you tell me when my stuff is coming – please!'

'Tressa, we're not giving you all your belongings right now,' she said slowly, picking her way back past the vegetables on the floor. 'We need to see how you're going to settle in first. You will get them back in time. Just be patient.'

'What right have you got to keep ma stuff?'

'We're not keeping it. By the way, I think we should say hello properly, don't you? I'm Beth. I'll be your keyworker while you're here.'

'How long will I be here?' It suddenly occurred to me that I didn't have any idea how long my warrant lasted.

'I believe your Section 69 is for three weeks,' said Beth.

I didn't know how to react to that news. After Beth had left, I just stared at the door after her. Three weeks of being locked in this room? I was serving time, just like a real prisoner. What was my crime? Telling the truth! I realised then that I had brought all this on myself. Jason had been right all along – I should never have told anyone. I was being punished for opening my big mouth and now I would just have to suffer. I crawled under the thin coverlet that night and watched as the electric blinds on the window were snapped shut. Beth came round one last time to announce that lights were going out in five minutes but I didn't really mind. I was ready to sleep. I closed my eyes and retreated into the world of unconsciousness. Whatever happened to me now, it was out of my control. There was nothing I could do about it anymore. Nothing at all.

I came round the next morning to hear the soft spatter of rain against my small window. For a minute, I just lay there, looking up at the drops trickling down the pane. I felt refreshed. For the first time in a very long time, since that time with Jason at my mum's house, I'd slept well. It was as if I'd left all my troubles at the door, with my bags, and finally I was free to relax. I smiled to myself then. Suddenly, I felt a gnawing at my insides – I was starving! I waited anxiously for Beth to bring me some food and when she did, I wolfed down everything: porridge, toast and yoghurt. All I wanted now was to get out of this bloody room!

It wasn't until 5pm that they finally came and got me. Beth and a male keyworker opened the door and invited me to come to dinner.

'I'm Matt,' said the man. He smiled at me and beckoned me out. Now that the door was open, I was almost afraid to walk through it. I was going to meet the other 'inmates'.

'Come on,' he laughed. 'Don't worry – we won't bite.'

Aye, it's not you I'm worried about, I thought to myself. Oh well – nothing for it now. It was out of my control. I walked slowly out, then Beth closed my door. They walked me up the corridor – Matt in front and Beth behind. We came to several doors along the corridor and each time, Matt swiped his keycard over a small panel at the side, which unlocked the door. I could see that every part of this unit was locked – you literally couldn't get anywhere without one of those cards.

The corridor eventually turned right and Matt swiped us into a dining room which was filled with kids at four large round tables.

The chattering stopped almost immediately as dozens of eyes turned towards me. I felt my cheeks flame with embarrassment and I looked to Matt who gestured towards a free seat at one of the tables. Each table had four seats, screwed down to the floor.

I slid into the plastic seat and looked down, only

occasionally lifting my eyes to take in my fellow diners. I felt so self-conscious at that point – I knew I was the 'new girl'. That's why they were all staring at me. I stole surreptitious glances left and right.

The kids there all looked quite young – in fact, the boy next to me couldn't have been more than eight or nine. It was a shock to see a child so little in a place like this. What on earth was *he* doing here?

Matt slid a plate in front of me – chicken with rice and black beans – and handed me a plastic knife and fork.

'Oh aye!' he said cheerily, when I shot him a questioning look. 'You get a knife out here. But they've all got to go back at the end of the meal!' Then he pointed towards a hatch where there were two sudsy bowls, obviously meant for our used cutlery and plates.

I tucked in enthusiastically – I don't know why but I was really hungry in this place. Maybe because there was nothing else to do! I was dying for a smoke but that was out of the question.

'Hi, I'm Sheila,' the girl next to me said brightly.

'Tressa,' I mumbled, darting a quick smile in her direction.

Sheila took it upon herself to make the rounds of introductions.

'Tressa – this is James and Gavin.' The boys raised their eyebrows in greeting.

'James, how old are you?' I asked the little boy next to me. His feet didn't even touch the floor.

'Seven, why? How old are you?'

'Fourteen.'

He nodded and his eyes slid down to the cuts on my arms,

the places where I'd hurt myself to take away the pain inside. For a moment I felt embarrassed, until I looked down at James's arms and saw that his were scarred as badly as mine – if not worse. My gaze lingered on the arms and suddenly I felt a terrible sadness welling up in me. Every single child at my table had cuts on their hands and arms.

It was a horrible realisation, but at the same time, I felt the tension in my body easing. I knew in that moment that none of the kids wanted to hurt me. Like me, they only wanted to hurt themselves.

'What are you in here for?' Sheila asked, through mouthfuls of rice.

'Absconding,' I told her. 'I kept running away and getting drunk.'

'I'm in for the same,' she grinned.

'Me too!' piped up Gavin.

'Yeah, and me,' said James. 'They got us now, though, eh Tressa?'

I laughed. I should have cried but I laughed. Because it was true – they had us now and none of us was going anywhere. So I guess I had to make the best of it. I finished most of my rice and chicken – which was delicious – and then they brought out dessert. Apple crumble and custard. It was the best thing I'd ever tasted!

Afterwards we went up one by one and put our plates and cutlery in the soapy plastic bowls. Matt was watching us carefully at the side of the hatch, making sure all our cutlery went in. We were then taken through to a living room with blue curtains and a dark blue carpet where we watched TV until 8pm. I sat in a corner, trying to be as quiet as possible, hoping to stay out of trouble. There were some older kids in the group –they looked about fifteen or sixteen – and I worried that I would look at someone the wrong way, provoking them. When Matt came to take me back to my room, he explained I was allowed a few of my belongings at a time. These he put in my room. I shrugged. There was no point arguing in here; it wasn't going to make any difference.

It didn't take long for me to get used to being in St Katherine's. Sheila and I became close and we had a small school in the unit where I could draw and paint. The classes were pretty easy and there was a big gym too so I could burn some of my energy. Sober now, I thought a lot about Annie – about how much I missed her. And I told the social workers I wanted to see her. I didn't want to go ahead with the adoption – it felt that it was being forced on me and wasn't what I wanted. So what if her dad was my brother? That wasn't her fault and it wasn't mine either. She was still my daughter and I loved her.

My mum came to see me a couple of times and I always looked forward to her visits. But whenever she came, she told me everything that was going on at home, and this always left me depressed and angry. At first, they had had me on 'observation' every ten minutes because of the self-harming and suicide attempts but this was quickly dropped when they saw that I wasn't trying to hurt myself. On the whole, I felt quite calm in St Katherine's. But the observations returned after my mum's visits.

I just couldn't understand why she stuck up for Jason. I tried to think it through but in the end, I kept coming back to the same thing: she should believe me. She should be on my side! The trial was coming up and I worried that this would only isolate me further from my family but there was nothing I could do about it. He had done this to himself!

Our routine in St Katherine's was pretty much the same every day, except on Saturdays when we were allowed to sleep in and then we'd have a fry-up for brunch. The food was really good in St Katherine's – we had a chef who made very healthy meals and I got used to eating well. Saturdays were the time for us to do our chores: cleaning our rooms, hoovering, dusting and washing. After three weeks, my Section 69 was extended for a further three months and though I felt trapped by the situation, I didn't mind too much because that week I got a TV in my room.

I can't say I enjoyed being there but I suppose, after the past few turbulent months, St Katherine's was a calm and peaceful period for me. I spoke to the psychiatrist once a week and I enjoyed some of the activities that were arranged for us like ice-skating, dance classes and cycling outings. I also enjoyed talking to Beth and Matt, who were both really nice.

'Am I ever going to get out of here?' I groaned to Beth one Saturday night. I'd done my make-up nicely that evening because I wanted to do something to make myself feel good – but there was no point. It wasn't like I was going out. I hadn't been out in months!

'You know, Tressa, you'll look back on this later in life and it will feel like just a short period of your time,' she said.

'You're joking!' I scoffed. 'It feels like years already!'

'I promise you, it won't feel like that when you're twenty.'

One night Beth brought in some old bridesmaid dresses she'd collected from her friends, and Sheila and I had a real laugh trying them all on. We giggled endlessly as we paraded around in the puffy, tulle skirts and tight, shimmering bodices.

It was fun to play dress-up – almost like being a kid again – and I found myself laughing in a way I hadn't done in years. Joyfully! There was something liberating about being in St Katherine's, a place where all the so-called 'bad' kids were sent. Here, we didn't judge each other. In our eyes, and to the credit of all the staff who worked there, we seemed okay to one another. I didn't feel like a 'bad' person. In here, around kids my age and without all the drink and the drugs, I could let myself believe that I was just like everyone else and nothing crappy had ever happened to me.

One day, I'd just made an apple pie in Home Economics at school when Beth came to find me. She said that Annie was on her way over to the unit for a visit. I was so excited, I nearly dropped the pie! I ran all the way to the living room. My daughter! I was breathless with anticipation. I hadn't seen her in months and I could barely sit still. I kept pacing the floor, biting my nails. When she finally toddled in, she clung to the back of her foster carer's legs.

I crouched down and flung my arms wide open: 'Baby!'

But instead of running and jumping into my cuddle as I expected, she only inched herself further behind the legs, a look of worried mistrust clouding her beautiful features.

'Hey, Annie!' I urged. 'Come to Mummy!'

But her bottom lip wobbled uncertainly and she looked up at the woman next to her.

'Mummy! Mummy!' she wailed, crying and holding her arms up to the foster carer.

My heart sank – she didn't recognise me. She was scared of

me! It hurt so much but I tried not to let it show. The foster carer smiled apologetically and I wanted to hit her right then. How dare she feel sorry for me! I didn't need her pity. I sat down on the chair and started talking to myself, trying to entice Annie towards me.

'What have I got here?' I babbled animatedly to myself. 'Is it a pie? I wonder what kind of pie it is. Is it a blueberry pie? Or a blackberry pie? Maybe it's a magic pie...'

On and on I went. It took a while but finally she came to me and we shared some of the apple pie I'd just made.

Afterwards in my room, I finally let the emotions of the day overtake me and softly cried into my pillow. The whole visit had been heartbreaking but it made me even more determined to get Annie back. I was her mother and I wanted to be the best mum I could possible be for her.

'We think you've made excellent progress in here,' Helen said on one of her visits in October. 'And we need to find an exit plan for you that builds on that progress.'

'Am I not going back into foster care?' I asked.

'No, we have found an excellent placement for you with Care Visions in Dumfries and Galloway. It's a wonderful place where you're going to get all the necessary support you need. Would you like to go and see it?'

'Okay.' I was finally beginning to trust social services. Though I'd hated being denied my freedom in St Katherine's, I could see that being sent there had almost certainly saved my life.

We had driven miles out of Edinburgh, down winding country lanes, until finally we arrived at a cottage at the end of a long path surrounded on either side by high, forested hills. It was called Roselands. 'I'm not fucking staying here!' I exploded when I got there.

A woman had come out of the cottage, introducing herself as Maggie. She looked like a Barbie doll – long, blonde hair extensions cascading down her back in ringlets, tons of make-up, high heels and perfectly manicured nails. She had a winning smile to match but even this strange doll-like woman couldn't distract me from one alarming fact.

'I'm away from everyone here!' I objected, waving my arms around. This was Dumfries and Galloway, several miles away from everyone I'd ever known in my life, but also, it was in the middle of nowhere! Beyond the hills was just mile after mile of open countryside – there wasn't another house for miles, let alone a shop, bus stop, café or school!

Maggie had already moved inside the cottage, insisting on showing us round the rooms.

'It's not even close to a shop!' I grumbled as I followed her up the stony path. 'What if I want to buy something?'

'Well, that's why we've got cars,' Maggie said simply. 'So we can get you from A to B.'

I kept quiet after that and let Maggie show me all the different parts of the house.

I seethed silently for the rest of the visit. It was only on the way back to St Katherine's that the penny finally dropped.

'You *want* me to be away from all my family and friends!' I said to Helen, who was driving us back in the fading daylight.

She kept her eyes on the road as she replied carefully: 'We're not trying to keep you away from anybody, Tressa. We just want what's best for you.'

'How is this best for me? You're keeping me in the middle

of nowhere, away from all the people I love and care about. Away from all my friends.'

Helen shot me an angry look.

'What? The friends who got drunk with you? The ones who told you to run away and stay out? Those friends? The people who let you get into such a state that we had to put you into a secure unit and never did anything to help?'

'What about my family?'

Helen didn't reply. She hated my family even more than my friends.

'Now I'll never have the chance to make things right with them,' I said bitterly. I had imagined that when I got out of St Katherine's, I could talk to Mum, Dad, Dionne and all my aunties and uncles. I could try to put my side of the story to them.

'Tressa, you haven't done anything wrong,' she sighed.

'Aye, that's not how they see it.'

'Well, that's not your problem. Look, Tressa, you have to try and focus on yourself for now. Don't worry so much about what everyone else thinks. You can't control their thoughts – but you can control your own life.'

It was dark when we finally arrived back to St Katherine's. *Another new start, another new home*, I thought to myself as I watched TV that night in the living room. How many more times did I have to start over?

Roselands

I sat up in my bed and stared out of the window – the last of the yellow-brown leaves broke free from their branches and were thrown about in the autumnal gusts. Occasional sheets of rain flew across the sky, whipping up more leaves and swaying the tops of the tall fir trees. It was a grey, cold day in late November but inside, I felt happy. I pulled my duvet up to my chin and watched the swirling leaves on the front path, dancing about in the changing breeze.

Watching the world outside from the cosiness of my bed made me feel even warmer. It was early morning, a time when I loved to just sit looking out of the window, watching nature's blustery performance. Out here in Roselands, my gaze could wander uninterrupted for miles around and after the confinement of St Katherine's, it felt wonderful to hear birds in the morning, watch the clouds scudding across the large, open sky, and marvel at all the busy squirrels and rabbits that made their home here. It was so different from everything I'd ever known. It was funny, magical, beautiful.

I'd been at Roselands for nearly a month and at first it had been a shock to be away from all the sights, sounds and smells of the city. Where were the late-night sirens blaring in the distance? The slamming of car doors? Shouts of kids on bikes wheeling up and down? Here it was always silent except at daybreak when the morning chorus of the birds broke through my dreams. At night Roselands was pitch black – no glaring orange streetlights, or pricks of light from the windows next door, just the vast empty darkness of the forest. Here, away from communal living, away from the dramas and stresses of the city, I felt my head starting to clear and a new calmness taking over. I knew now I didn't want to die – I didn't want to hurt myself at all. And that meant no cutting, no drugs and no drinking. It felt like all that stuff was in the past, not the future.

'I know that the drinking was hurting me,' I told Maggie one evening, as we sat on the sofas in the living room, a soft peachy glow lighting the room from two small table lamps. I had a hot water bottle tucked under my arms and a tartan rug pulled over my knees. She had her feet up on the floral footrest and was applying a new coat of polish to her nails.

'Aye,' she nodded, as she carefully painted the bright pink lines on the tips of each finger. At first there had been another boy living here but he left a week after I arrived. It was just as well, as during our first chat he'd invited me to rob a shop with him. I'd just laughed – we were miles away from any shop! It was pure fantasy. Still, I was glad when he left. I knew this was my chance to make a better life for myself and I didn't want to blow it. I wanted to stay on course.

'I was just trying to escape from reality,' I went on. 'I didn't want to be me anymore. It just felt too hard.'

'And now?' Maggie asked sweetly.

'And now… Now it's getting easier,' I nodded to myself. 'Aye, it's definitely not as hard. I'm thinking more clearly. I don't want to escape.'

I'd turned fifteen just before the move to Roselands and it felt that with every month that passed, I was growing up. I looked back at the scared little girl who gave birth to Annie and I felt sorry for her. All those hopes she had of raising her little girl with her mum by her side – they were just dreams! I smiled ruefully to myself. For the first time, I was beginning to see that what had happened to me wasn't all my fault. My mum's and dad's lives had been too chaotic, too focused on the wrong things. I'd been raped since the age of seven – why had nobody noticed? Why had it gone on so long? In the past I had always made excuses for my mum, always said that she was doing her best but as time went on and I began to see the choices she made in a clearer light, I realised that she didn't always try her best. There were times she was meant to come and see me in St Katherine's and she never turned up. Just like those contact meetings with Ollie and Kai. She was meant to come and visit me here in Roselands but she hadn't managed it yet. I knew that Mum's choice to support Jason had also damaged me severely. I could see that now. It hurt me so much that she had sided with him but I couldn't change her mind. I couldn't change her at all. Part of coming to terms with my past was learning to accept the fact that I couldn't run her life for her, that I had to look after myself instead of protecting her all the time. If she messed up, she would have to live with the consequences. As much as it hurt – and as much as it impacted on my own life – I knew that this was a big step I had to take. Breaking free was my only hope.

'You're strong, you are!' Maggie remarked one day as we were unloading the week's shopping in the kitchen. Maggie lived in the house with me in a bedroom on the lower floor. And when she wasn't around, there was always another carer.

The comment seemed to come out of thin air. We'd talked a lot in the last month – there wasn't much choice as there weren't many other people to talk to. But I didn't understand why she suddenly said this.

'What do you mean?' I asked, confused. I thought she was referring to the fact that I'd carried in three bags of shopping.

'I mean, you've been through a lot and look at you! You've coped so well. You've got a lot more strength than you give yourself credit for.'

I thought about this. In some ways, I could see she was right. I was stronger than I thought. I always thought that I needed my family, that I couldn't cope without them. Well, that wasn't true. I could stand on my own two feet and here, in Roselands, I was given the confidence and freedom to build up that strength.

Before I started at Dumfries High School in January 2009, Maggie and I went out a lot. Sometimes another member of staff would come if Maggie was off that day. We went to the cinema, swimming and ice-skating, and took long trips in to the countryside. But best of all, I started horse riding at the local stables. I'd always adored animals but I'd never visited stables before. I loved being around the horses – they were such magnificent, gorgeous creatures.

'Here, how do you fancy a Saturday job?' Jan, the owner of the stables, asked me one day after she caught me stroking the nose of one of my favorite piebald ponies. I liked to hang around at the end of my lessons, just petting and talking to the animals.

'Are you serious?' I asked, excited.

'Sure, we always need help mucking out so if you want to come and work on Saturdays, we'll give you your lessons for free.'

It was the most wonderful offer I'd ever had. From that day, I became a regular at the stables and even after I started at my new school, I'd race down there two or three times a week after my classes to be around the horses.

Around the animals and nature, I felt normal. Life was uncomplicated. There were no dramas, no worries and no demands on me. I could just be an ordinary kid again and worry about ordinary kid stuff. The horses didn't judge me; they didn't ask anything of me – they were simple but noble animals and I felt relaxed around them. I enjoyed being back in school too – it had been ages since I'd been in a proper classroom and I concentrated hard during lesson time. I had to! I was studying so many subjects: History, Biology, Maths, English, Home Ec. and, of course, Art. I was nervous at first about joining a new school but my keyworkers helped me to talk through my worries. We even put together a rehearsed 'script' for when other kids asked about my background and why I was there. I didn't lie but in the script I missed out some of the essential facts that might identify me, like the abuse by Jason, the fact that I had been a young mum and other stuff. I even went by my mum's surname, Tallons, instead of Middleton so that people wouldn't immediately recognise me as 'the youngest mum in Scotland'. I wanted to be able to start at my new school without the past holding me back and defining me. I wanted just to be accepted for who I was. In fact, the kids were all really nice and it didn't take long for me to make new friends – friends my age who didn't go out drinking and smoking for fun. These were friends who enjoyed normal activities like going to the cinema, the ice rink or the swimming pool.

At the end of each week I was given my pocket money and on Saturdays Maggie or another carer drove me into town to spend it. Sometimes I bought CDs but I spent a lot of my money on nice pencils and good paper for drawing. I loved sitting in the living room, looking out the window and trying to sketch the birds in the garden or the trees outside. Here, for the first time, I felt that maybe I could have a proper life. A life free from drink, drugs and abuse. I had been in such a dark and dreadful place before the move to Roselands that I hadn't realised to what extent it had been caused by my circumstances.

What if I'd been born into this world? I wondered to myself as I shovelled hay around the stables one day. *What if I'd had different parents? What if my brother hadn't started abusing me at seven and I'd not been given hash and booze from such a young age? What if I'd grown up in the fresh air of the countryside where there were no temptations, just healthy happy activities like ice-skating and horse riding? Would it have been different?* Before my move here, I hadn't been able to imagine what a good life might look like for me. I'd just never experienced it. Now my eyes were opened and I realised that I had a chance to start again. Properly this time.

Now one thought dominated all others: I wanted Annie back. In the past year I'd lost so much time with her and I yearned to have her back in my arms. I kept pictures of her all over my walls and even had a little yellow babygro of hers which I slept with under my pillow.

It turned out that Jan, who ran the stables, was also good with legal stuff and she helped to find me a lawyer to fight the adoption case. She helped me to fill out the forms so that I could one day be reunited with my daughter for good.

I finally understood why the social workers had taken her away – I was a mess at the time and it had been for her own good. But now I was back on course and I wanted to give her this life! I wanted her to grow up breathing the fresh, clean air of the countryside, walking through hills and forests, riding along the beautiful valleys and watching the changing seasons outside the window. If I could give her this childhood, this life, this world, then she would be happy. And that's all I wanted.

In April 2009, I prepared to see her in one of my rare contact visits at Bathgate Social Centre. I'd been looking forward to this day for weeks. That morning I put on my best navy jeans and my favourite woollen green jumper. Then I carefully applied my make-up in the bathroom mirror the way Maggie had shown me – not too much, not too little. I hummed happily to myself as I examined my reflection. Gone were the purple bags under my eyes, the blotchy skin and the red eyes. My skin was clear, my cheeks had a rosy glow, my hair looked thick and healthy, and I was no longer stick-thin but nicely rounded in the right places. Country living definitely suited me. I wanted to look my best for my daughter and as I looked closely at my reflection that day, I smiled at myself. Yes, here was a mother Annie could be proud of at last! My heart soared as we left that day for the centre, half an hour's drive away. She was not yet three years old but I knew that this could be the start of our new life together.

Little did I realise it would be the last time I ever saw her.

CHAPTER 18

Last Contact

'Come here, baby!' I cooed, squatting down on the floor with my arms open wide. 'Come on. Come to Mummy!'

Annie looked wide-eyed at me and then tugged nervously on the trousers of her foster mother. A second later her face crumpled into tears and she started wailing: 'Mummy! Mummy!'

'Aye, I'm your Mummy too,' I smiled hopefully. 'I'm your Tummy Mummy. Are yous not going to come and say hello?'

Annie shook her head and put her face against the foster carer's legs, a new lady – one I'd not seen before. She was a little older than the last one, perhaps in her mid-thirties, with short blonde hair and glasses. Her and her husband had applied to adopt Annie.

'I'm sorry,' she said, twisting round to unhook Annie's strong little fingers from her legs. 'It's been a long car journey.

She's probably quite tired.' She tried to pull Annie away but she clung on, determined.

I stood up, angry now.

'Why do her trousers have a hole in them?' I asked, as I appraised the state of my daughter. 'And look at her hair! It's all over the place!'

Everything felt wrong today. Our contact had been arranged in the Bathgate Social Centre's conference room – a large, featureless space with no toys or sofas. It felt bleak and intimidating. I bit down hard on my lip – poor Annie! I'd feel scared too if I was her! They could have at least arranged for us to meet somewhere that was warm and welcoming.

'We've just been to the zoo,' the foster carer explained. 'She fell over and made a hole in the knee – it's not normally like that.'

'Aye, but you could have made her look nice for her contact,' I fumed. I wasn't really annoyed with the way she looked, of course; I was just frustrated and disappointed by the whole situation.

I tried my best – for an hour I attempted to engage Annie by showing her some of the cards I'd made her. I'd even drawn and coloured a Winnie the Pooh for her, which I tried to give her. But she spent the whole time crying for her foster parents. I'd been looking forward to this so much and now I realised that Annie barely knew who I was. It broke my heart. In the whole time we were together, she never called me Mummy once.

'What are you thinking?' Helen asked me on the drive back to Roselands that afternoon. I'd been quiet a long time, just staring out of the window.

'She doesn't know me,' I sighed. 'She doesn't want to be with me.'

Helen stayed quiet.

'I never thought she wouldn't recognise me,' I added. The tears now broke free and rolled down my cheeks. I brushed them away with my sleeve. 'It's not fair! I never had a chance!'

Helen remained silent – but then after a while, she asked, 'Are you thinking about what you might do next?'

'Aye. Aye, I am.'

I thought long and hard about the adoption. For the next few nights I lay awake in my bed, wondering whether or not I was doing the right thing. Annie had already had so many different carers. What sort of a life would she have if I kept fighting? The judge had told me at the last hearing that I was being selfish – he said that if I carried on fighting the adoption then I might not get Annie back for another four years. That was four more years of instability for her, four more years of being moved from pillar to post, never feeling settled. That was no life; I knew that. I knew from my own experience what it felt like to go from one place to the next, never being able to fully relax.

I couldn't do that to her.

As much as it killed me, I knew I had to do the right thing by my daughter. The foster parents who wanted to adopt her were good people, kind people, and they had good jobs and a stable home life.

That week my emotions swung about all over the place. I was at times teary and then full of rage. Sometimes it made my blood boil just to think of those foster carers – why did they want my child?

What right did they have to take my daughter away?

I envied their comfortable lives, their jobs, home, good clothes, twice-yearly foreign holidays... I'd never even left Scotland!

They had it all – why did they need to take my daughter as well?

But eventually my fury ran out and I'd throw myself onto the bed, weeping with grief. I had lost my daughter – it wasn't their fault. She didn't need me; she didn't even know who I was. I couldn't give her the life she deserved and they could. Worse, if I kept trying, I would be denying her any sort of life. I would be condemning her to a childhood fraught with instability, uncertainty and constant change. That was the truth of the matter.

So a week after the contact with Annie, I called my lawyer and told him to drop the contest of the adoption. It was one of the hardest calls I've ever made and that night I felt so awful I just wanted to get horribly drunk. The papers were delivered to me two days later and I signed them, with a very heavy heart.

Everyone said I was doing the right thing – Helen, Maggie, Jan, all my social workers. But it was still so hard.

'You can see her one last time,' Helen offered over the phone the next day. 'You have that option.'

But I couldn't bear it.

'No,' I whispered. 'No, I don't think so. I don't think that would do either of us any good.'

I recalled the last contact. Saying goodbye to her that time had been one of the most depressing moments of my life. My arms ached for a cuddle, my whole body felt empty. I was desperate for that one bit of physical contact with her, the daughter I'd carried around in my body, the one I'd talked to in the womb, the precious person I'd fallen in love with the moment she arrived. The one I'd worried over, cried over, sung to and clung to – I needed to feel her against me.

But when it came to leaving me, she only offered the briefest and most reluctant of hugs – an exquisite and awful moment all at the same time. I felt my heart shatter as she ran away from me.

No, I couldn't go through all of that again.

'Tressa, be strong,' said Helen. 'You're being so brave and making such a mature decision. I know you're going through a lot of turmoil but it will get better.'

'Will I get contact?' I asked hopefully.

'Letters,' she said. 'Twice a year.'

I couldn't face going to school the next day so I stayed in bed. I didn't want to move at all. Maggie tried to entice me up with offers of toasted cheese sandwiches and cups of tea but her efforts were wasted. I didn't want to get up because I was afraid of what I might do. I knew what I wanted to do – I wanted to find a razor and cut myself. It felt like the only way of relieving the terrible pain inside.

For three days I stayed in my room. Eventually, Maggie suggested I go to the stables to spend some time with the horses. She thought that would make me feel better. But when Jan came and found me weeping in a corner of one of the stables, she lifted me up and took me back to her place. I cried like a baby in her arms.

'What can I do?' she asked, as she held me and smoothed

the hair away from my damp cheeks. 'What can I do to make this better?'

'I don't know,' I sobbed. 'I don't know. I want my mum. I want to speak to my mum.'

'Okay, okay,' she soothed, standing up purposefully. She went to get the cordless phone from the hallway. 'We'll get your mum on the phone.'

It was probably the worst thing I could have done.

'What the fuck!' Mum screamed when I told her about the adoption. 'That's my grandkid as well! Did you ever think of that? I'm not going to see her again.'

'How do you think I feel?' I whispered in a small voice.

'I'm sure you feel better!' she railed. 'Oh aye! It's all right for you now you've got your new life and nothing to get in your way!'

By the time I came off the phone I was hysterical. Jan quickly made a call to Roselands and Maggie came to pick me up.

'I'm sorry!' she said as Maggie bustled in. 'I didn't know! I thought it would help. She said she wanted to ring her mum.'

'You weren't to know,' Maggie said as she swept me up and led me to the car outside. I hardly knew where I was anymore. I let Maggie drive me back, and then lead me upstairs to bed and tuck me up like a little girl. The next few days were a blur – I found myself staring for hours at photos of Annie, tracing with my finger the outline of her chubby cheeks, examining the baby book I had started for her when she was first born. I spread out on my bed all the old baby clothes I'd kept and lay down on them, breathing in their fading baby scent.

When it got too much, I went into the kitchen, stole a small knife and used it to slash at my arms. It was the only thing that helped take the pain away. And the guilt. The terrible, agonising, all-consuming guilt that made my stomach churn. It infected me, this guilt, like a disease. I was paralysed by the tingling in my fingers and toes – by the thoughts that swarmed round and round in my head.

You've let her down. All those promises you made to her, you didn't keep any of them. You're meant to be her mother! What kind of mother are you? You're useless, stupid, unworthy.

Even as the thoughts attacked my mind, I was bombarded with flashbacks from the brickyard, from all those terrible times my brother had raped me. It felt like all the worst things in my life were coming back to me then, just as I was at my lowest ebb.

The carers and Roselands staff all did their best to comfort me. They really tried. They knew what my mum was like, they knew she wouldn't put my feelings first, and I wondered even if they'd been expecting this at some point. Until that call from Jan's place, they'd tried to discourage me from making contact with my mum. They said I needed time to sort out my own emotions before trying to deal with hers. In my heart I knew I was doing the right thing for Annie; I knew it was the best thing for her but it didn't make it any easier. My dad was no better – when I told him, he went mad too. How could I tell them that I'd done it out of love? How could they understand? Mum had chosen to keep all of us kids even when it was clear she couldn't look after us properly. Even after everything that happened, she thought we were better off living with her.

'She'll never get it,' Helen sighed to me at our next meeting.

'Your mum will never understand this – because it is the ultimate act of sacrifice by a truly loving mother.'

'She loved us all!' I was always ready to defend my mum.

'Aye, but was it enough?' Helen said gently.

Once I was up and out of bed, the social workers and carers at Roselands arranged a whirlwind of activities. They organised a day for Dionne to come and visit me and they took us both ice-skating. It was lovely. I'd never been skating with her before and it was so nice to do something fun together. But more than that, it felt nice to be with my family again. Out in Roselands on my own, I really felt so alone. I'd lost Annie and of course I didn't see the rest of the family. As far as I knew, they all hated me anyway – first for telling the police about Jason and secondly for giving up Annie. But Dionne was more forgiving – I tried to explain to her what had happened, the reason I couldn't keep fighting the adoption, and though it made her sad, I think she saw that I had Annie's best interests at heart. It meant so much that she understood.

There were other trips too – to the cinema, to Carlisle, to Laser Quest. Maggie took me to the salon and insisted on paying to get my hair and nails done. It felt nice that she was doing something for me and I tried to stay focused in school as much as possible. They all kept me busy, trying to stop me dwelling too much on the adoption. Eventually, after a couple of months, the cutting stopped and I managed to go to bed without crying every night.

At the end of June I left school and applied for a job as a chambermaid at a local country house hotel. I was surprised and delighted when the call came through to say I'd got the job. By now another girl, Chase, had moved into Roselands with me, and we had become good friends. She also got a job at the hotel and we got dropped off there every morning at 8.30am. Since we couldn't get into the guests' rooms until after 10am, we were allowed first to have the leftovers from the breakfast buffet. Then we cleaned the downstairs before tackling each room. I really enjoyed the work and it was nice to meet the other girls there.

After a day's work at the hotel, I'd go straight to Jan's place to help with the horses – mucking out and getting them ready for the lessons. At the end of each week I got a huge thrill from opening my wage packet. It was more money than I'd ever had in my life and at first, the idea of having £200 scared me so I asked Maggie to keep it for me so that I wasn't tempted to spend all of it at once. Still, I treated myself to some new clothes and even bought some new stuff for my wee brothers and sisters.

Things seemed to be going okay until the court case came up at the beginning of July. Jason had pleaded guilty in the end because of the DNA evidence but on the day of the sentencing at Glasgow Crown Court, Mum called me on my mobile.

'There's a mob!' she screeched down the line. 'A mob of 300 people standing outside ma house going mental!'

'What? What do you mean?' My heart started to race.

'I mean that they're out there and they're going to attack us!' she yelled. 'I'm going to have to get a police escort. I'm freaking out here!'

I was a bag of nerves all day long – what if they attacked my mum? What if they hurt her? I didn't want any of this. I had always wanted to retract my statement after giving it to the police but it was out of my hands. The DNA evidence had proved there was a rape and Jason didn't have any choice but to plead guilty.

It was my mum who called me with the result.

'Jason's been jailed,' she said in a dull voice. She sounded exhausted.

'Oh, I'm sorry,' I told her. I really was. I didn't want him to go to jail. I didn't want to cause any more problems. It felt like I was ruining everyone's lives and I didn't know how to fix it.

'On his birthday too!' she added, twisting the knife just that bit further. 'You know, they chucked a bottle at me when I came out of the house.'

'I'm sorry,' I said again. I knew it sounded lame but I didn't know what else to say.

'And I've got no money neither,' she said.

'I'll send you something,' I said quickly. 'I'll send you ma wages this week.'

'Yeah, alright,' she said and hung up.

I felt really bad for her. I knew I shouldn't but she was my mum! I hated to think that I was the cause of all this hurt. That night I watched the news and saw Jason walking into the court with his hoodie pulled right up to his cap to obscure his face. They said he had raped me while high on crack cocaine. His lawyer had argued for a reduced sentence, claiming he'd not had a normal upbringing, that there was no moral framework in his house, no parental guidance. *Poor Mum*, I thought. It was bad enough for her going through all of this but now everyone would blame her for what Jason did!

But the judge hadn't been persuaded. She said Jason had made excuses for his actions, blaming drink, drugs and even me for starting it! That made my blood boil – I mean, it was one thing to try and deny what he'd done. It was another to blame the victim.

The judge said there was a high risk he would commit further crimes in the future and if he'd not pled guilty he would get five years. As it was, she gave him three years followed by a two-year supervision order. Then they showed the angry crowds outside my mum's house in Livingston and the moment Jason had come out, surrounded by police to stop him getting hurt. Despite everything, I felt for him then. I knew that he deserved it but I didn't want him to go to jail. He was still my brother after all. I found it so hard to explain how I felt to all the social workers and counsellors. They all expected me to be pleased, to hate Jason. But I couldn't. It was all so mixed-up.

I thought Victim Support might help but they were only interested in the compensation.

'I don't want any bloody money!' I told them bitterly. It felt wrong – why should I get money out of this horrible situation when my brother was in jail, my wee brothers and sister in care, and my whole family in tatters? The money would just be a constant reminder of everything that had happened.

'We should still put in the forms,' the lady on the phone insisted. 'You might change your mind in a few years. And if you really don't want the money, then it could be put into a trust fund for Annie some time in the future.'

That made me think – I felt like I'd failed my daughter in so many ways. Perhaps in this one way I could give her something that would help her make her way in the world. Perhaps with a secure financial future she would have some opportunities in her life. I couldn't give her much but I supposed this was one thing.

'Okay,' I agreed. 'Let's do the forms.'

For the rest of the summer, I tried to put the court case behind me. It wasn't easy. For a few weeks my mum refused to speak to me. She was too upset.

When we finally started talking again, I tried to bring up Jason.

'Just forget about it,' she snapped. 'I don't want to talk about it.'

'But Mum…'

'I said forget it! I'm not taking anyone's side, okay? I just… I just can't talk about it. I love you both. You're both my children.'

There was a long silence then.

'Are you getting by alright, Mum?' I asked sadly, emotion swelling in my chest.

'Aye, aye…'

'Do you want me to send you some money?'

'Aye.'

CHAPTER 19

Dad

'Happy birthday, darling!' Dad yelled, taking me in a great big bear hug and planting a sloppy kiss on my cheek.

'Thanks, Dad,' I smiled, slightly embarrassed but also quietly pleased.

'Look at yous!' he smiled, giving me an affectionate squeeze. 'You're doing well, aren't you? I'm proud of you, Tressa. Cheers!'

He held up a bottle of Budweiser and tipped his head back to take a long swig. It was my sixteenth birthday and Dad had taken me for a special night out. I looked around me at the flashing lights in the dark, cavernous club and felt happy. People were dancing, joking around, flirting, snogging even – this was like a world away from my quiet life in Roselands. It was so nice to share some time with my dad and it really felt, for the first time in my life, that he cared.

Over the summer, Dad and I had spoken lots on the phone. I'd told him about my life in Roselands, my job, the stables and the new friends I'd made there. I also told him I was missing seeing my family. He'd invited me to come and spend the weekend with him in Pumpherston. I'd never spent much time with my dad so it felt wonderful that he was reaching out to me. I needed it. I needed it so much. After everything I'd lost, it felt like I was finally getting some contact back with my family.

But I barely knew Dad – from my past I had fixed ideas that he was just the bloke who used to batter my mum. But the more time I spent with him, the more I realized that he was a really nice bloke and it was clear his violent days were behind him. He had recently split up with his girlfriend Maria so he had a spare room in the house for me. Dad really liked to have a good time and, sensing I'd been at a very low ebb following the adoption and court case, he seemed determined I should have a good time too. He liked a drink and, it turned out, a few other things besides: coke, ecstasy, speed. But he wasn't a down person – once he was partying, he was the best person to be around and loads of fun. I liked going to see him and after a couple of visits he asked if I'd like to move in.

Helen urged me not to – in fact, every single one of my care workers said it was a bad idea.

'He'll let you down again,' she warned. 'Just like he has so many times before – and you'll get hurt, Tressa. I'm just worried for you, worried that all the good work you've done to improve your life will go out the window. What about your job, for example?'

'I can get a job up there,' I said. 'Look, I really want to do this, Helen. I don't know my dad! I want to get to know him. It feels like I've got a chance here and I just want to take it.'

'He's still drinking, Tressa,' she said, shaking her head. 'I don't want you to get dragged into all of that again – the drinking, substance abuse, the partying. You're safe here – you've got good things in your life…'

'I've got to be free to make my own choices!' I exploded. 'I've had everything decided for me for the last five years: where I live, where I go to school, who I can see, who I can't see. I'm sick of it! I want to make my own decisions and if I decide to have a drink that's ma choice now. I've proved to you all that I'm okay now. I'm sixteen. What more do I have to do? It's about time I lived my own life.'

'Okay, okay,' Helen put her hands up to me, as if surrendering. 'You're right. You are free to make your own choices. If you want to go and live with your dad, fine – we'll support you. But we'll keep your place at Roselands. That will be there for you just in case things don't work out.'

So just before my sixteenth birthday, I gave up my job at the hotel and moved into my dad's spare room. He made me feel very welcome, taking me out, giving me my own cupboard space in the kitchen and clearing out all the drawers for my stuff. Two weeks later he took me clubbing for my birthday. It was the first time I'd been to a nightclub and I loved it! That night he introduced me to all his friends and we danced till the early hours. I met a nice bloke that night, Adam. He was a bit older than me but we got on really well.

The next morning the staff at Roselands called to make sure I was alright. They called me every morning and every evening to make sure I was safe.

'You don't have to keep ringing me like this,' I said.

'Aye, we do,' Maggie said. 'Look, why don't you come back here for a few days? I've got a birthday present for you and we'll go to the salon to get our nails done. We'll cook together!'

She knew I loved cooking and I'll admit it sounded good. Dad didn't exactly eat regular meals, like I had become used to.

'Okay,' I smiled. 'I'll come back at the weekend.'

For a few months everything went well. Dad and I got along really well together and every now and then I'd pop back to Roselands for some healthy food and to catch up with Maggie and all my friends there. It felt like for the first time I was building a proper relationship with my dad.

'I always called to check on you, you know,' he told me one night when we discussed my time in St Katherine's. I'd told him how it felt being locked up there, almost like I was being punished for what Jason had done to me. I'd had so few family visits it felt like everyone had abandoned me.

'Aye, but you never came to see me,' I said.

'It was hard, Tressa love,' he said, scratching his head. 'I had ma own issues. And your mother, well, she never makes things easy. But I never stopped loving you, you know. I never stopped loving any of you.'

I started seeing Adam regularly, and he came and stayed a lot at my dad's place. He was the first real boyfriend I'd had and it was nice to feel that I had two people in my life who cared about me very much. But in the middle of December, when Dad and Maria got back together, everything changed. She came back to live in the house and it was clear from the start that she felt I was an unwelcome addition to the household.

She was tetchy and offhand with me, always complaining about Adam coming round. I didn't understand why and I tried my best to make myself useful around the house, offering to do the cleaning and washing up. When the place looked like it needed sprucing up, I'd do the hoovering, the cleaning and the dusting – after all, I'd done it for a job so I was quite good at it by then.

It all came to a head on New Year's Eve. Adam and I had been out drinking the night before and that evening I lay on the sofa with my head in his lap, fighting back the urge to throw up, while we watched the Hogmanay celebrations on the telly. Half an hour earlier Dad had gone out and come back with a Chinese takeaway for him and Maria. It annoyed me that he hadn't even offered to get Adam and me some too. Now that Maria was back, it seemed like I didn't matter anymore.

They tucked into the chow mein and stir fried rice enthusiastically but as the sweet and sour smell hit my nostrils, I felt bile rising in my throat again. I really did not feel well at all.

'Here, Tressa!' Dad called out to me, holding up his bottle of Bacardi. 'You want some of this?'

I couldn't think of anything worse at that moment.

'No, ta,' I replied, barely looking over at him.

Maria shot me a dirty look and then spoke to my dad: 'What's wrong with her tonight? What's she got a face like a slapped arse for?'

'Aye, what the fuck's up with you?' Dad was annoyed too now. 'Why are you being like this?'

'Like what?' I groaned. 'Nothing's up – just leave me alone!'

'I'll leave you alone, you ungrateful wee bastard!' Dad

snapped back. 'What do you have to lie around here in a foul mood on sodding New Year's Eve, killing everyone's good time!'

'I'm not in a mood,' I sat up, angry now. 'I'm just not well.'

'Aye, she's going to be sitting there all night with that face on her!' Maria said to my dad, jabbing her thumb in my direction. 'That miserable wee bitch is going to make us all suffer!'

I couldn't listen to any more of this. I jumped up and stormed out. How dare she talk to me like that! And worse, Dad had sided with her over me. It seemed like he was always willing to take her side these days. Bloody Adam hadn't said a word the whole time.

I went through to the bedroom and started throwing things into a bag. I was livid with them both but especially my dad. After all his talk about trying to build a new relationship, about starting again, he'd treated me like an unwelcome intruder the moment his girlfriend had come back. I clearly hadn't meant that much to him if he could toss me aside so easily. I shook with rage as I opened drawer after drawer, turning them out into the bag I had placed on the bed. I really didn't know what the plan was – all I knew was that I didn't feel welcome at my dad's anymore. It was nearly 10pm – too late to try and get back to Roselands.

For God's sake, it was New Year's Eve! Where on earth did I think I could go at this time on New Year's Eve? I hesitated for a moment and looked at the stuff in the bag. *Was this really such a good idea?*

At that moment Dad came thundering through to the room and when he saw my bag of clothes on the bed, he looked utterly shocked. And then his expression changed – he was enraged!

'What is this?' he hollered. 'Is that you fucking going then?'

He looked really mad: his eyes were bulging and his face went beetroot-red. I could see the little red veins popping out of his neck as he screamed: 'GO ON THEN – GO! FUCKING LEAVE! I DON'T WANT YOU HERE NO MORE'S ANYWAYS.'

'Yeah, I got that message,' I muttered as I quickly closed my bag and picked it up by the handles.

'Adam, are you coming?' I said as I strode through the living room with my bag of stuff. I hadn't even had time to put my shoes on – I was still in my slippers!

He looked up at me from the TV then, a confused expression passing over his face.

'Coming where?' he said.

'Just coming!' I said, clamping my mouth down, willing him to just follow me out the door.

Come on Adam! Follow me out – I don't want to go alone. Please!

But I wasn't going to beg – he had to want to come with me. However, I could see that he clearly thought I'd gone mad at that moment. I wanted him to jump up and urge me not to leave, to wrestle my bags off me and take me through to the bedroom for some soothing words of comfort and reassurance. But no, nothing like that happened.

'Er… No, you're alright,' he said. 'I think I'll stay here.'

'Right then,' I stomped to the door. 'Fair enough.'

On the street, I pondered my options. At that moment, I knew that the only place where I would be reasonably welcome at this hour was my mum's. I knocked at the door of a neighbour and luckily Phil answered – he was friends with my dad and I'd got to know him a bit these past few months. He was obviously shocked to see me but I hurriedly explained that I'd had a fight with my dad and asked if he could give me a lift to my mum's place.

'Aye,' he said, taking note of the fact that I was still wearing my slippers. 'I could do that but are you sure you don't want to just kip down here tonight? I'm sure it'll all blow over with your dad in the morning.'

'No, please Phil,' I said, nearly crying now. I just wanted to get as far away from Dad as possible. 'I'd really like to go to my mum's. Please!'

So he got his keys and we took the short drive to where my mum was living. She had recently moved into a flat in Livingston where her boyfriend Billy had been living for many years. I rang the bell and banged on the door but despite seeing all the lights were on, nobody came to answer. We waited around for a while, hugging ourselves against the cold, but nothing happened.

'I know,' I told him. 'I could go to my aunty Joanne's and get the key from her.'

So that's what I did. It turned out that Aunty Joanne was out for the night but Alex and his girlfriend Vanessa were there and they had Mum's front door key.

Phil and I went back to Billy's and I let myself in the front door. I walked through the dirty living room to the bedroom, where I saw Mum and her new boyfriend Billy passed out on the bed together.

It wasn't a proper sleep, I could see that. It was the sleep of two people who were utterly gone on something.

'Are you gonna be okay here?' Phil called uncertainly from the front door. I felt bad, making him run around town with me like this on New Year's Eve. I couldn't put him out any further.

'Oh aye,' I called back, putting a chirpy note in my voice that I definitely did not feel.

'Are you sure? I could take you back to your dad's if you like?'

'No, really,' I smiled as I came to the door. 'You've been great – thank you. I'll be fine.'

'Oh, okay then,' he said, hesitating. I could see he didn't like the look of the place. Just a quick glimpse into the lounge from the doorway revealed piles of dirty plates, empty bottles, week-old abandoned takeaways, overflowing ashtrays and all sorts of bits of foils and bags that had clearly been used for kit. I didn't care – I didn't plan to be here long. Just the one night and then I'd head back to Dumfries. I had to admit that living with my dad hadn't worked out as I'd imagined it. I'd get a train back tomorrow, I told myself, and pick up where I'd left off in Roselands, with my job and the stables.

Phil hopped from one foot to another, hands thrust deep into his pockets against the biting winter chill.

'Well, if you're sure I'll be on my way then,' he said.

'Okay. Thanks again, Phil,' I smiled.

'Nae bother. Cheerio.'

'Bye! Oh, and Phil...?'

'Aye?'

'Happy New Year!'

'Yeah, and Happy New Year to you, Tressa. Hope it's a good one.'

Aye, me too, I thought, as I picked my way across the dirt and clutter in the living room. I cleared a space on the largest sofa, lay down and pulled my coat over me for a blanket. What a way to start the year!

CHAPTER 20

Mum Again

'Oh, hello,' Mum drawled in a deep, not-yet-awake voice when she finally surfaced the next day at about 11am. I'd been up for hours already, tidying, clearing away, throwing out rubbish, washing up and wiping down surfaces. I'd woken up to the sight and smell of a mouldy plate of curry studded with fag ends next to my face and had decided in that moment that there was no way I was going to leave without making this place a little nicer for my mum.

I'd already managed a couple of hours and the place was looking a million times better, when Mum wandered into the kitchen in her dressing gown. If she was pleased to see me, she didn't let on. She didn't even seem that surprised.

'I thought I heard something last night,' she yawned as she flicked on the kettle. 'Was that you ringing the doorbell?'

'Aye,' I said, my hands still in a hot bowl of washing up. 'I thought you were completely out for the count.'

'I was,' Mum said, leaning heavily on the kitchen counter. 'Billy and I got our meds the day before yesterday. I think we took about a month's worth in two nights. I was fucking wrecked!'

I placed the last of the plates on the draining board and took the plug out of the sink. Then I turned to face Mum properly. She looked awful. It had been months since I'd last seen her and I was shocked at how quickly she'd deteriorated. She had always been thin but now she was drawn, haggard and skeletal. It seemed like she'd aged ten years in the past ten months. My heart crumbled at that moment – I wanted to go over and hug her and make everything better. I could see that nothing had improved in her life – if anything, it was much, much worse. Apart from a bed, TV, sofa and one coffee table, there wasn't a stick of furniture in the house. Whatever they'd once owned had clearly been sold for drugs. The laminate floor in the kitchen was full of holes and there wasn't any flooring at all in the hallway. The walls were so filthy and grimy that they were actually black in places and the whole flat stank of urine. This was no more than a doss house. Still, I wanted to be here. I wanted to be with my mum.

'So what happened then?' she asked, picking up a packet of baccy and some papers. I could tell from her wheezy voice and the way she struggled for each breath that her asthma was back and worse than ever.

'I had a fight with Dad,' I said. 'I got a lift here from his neighbour and Alex gave me the keys. That alright?'

'Oh aye, it's fine by me,' she said, rolling herself a cigarette. 'You can kip here if you like. I don't mind.'

Just then Billy wandered through the corridor to the

bathroom. He was like a zombie, trudging heavily, head down, barely conscious.

'He'll be alright too,' Mum said, popping the fag in her mouth.

I wanted to say something to her then. I wanted to tell her how sorry I was about Jason going to jail, about all the abuse she'd suffered as a result. I wanted to tell her I wasn't angry with her and that I didn't blame her for any of it.

'Mum, look...' I started. But before I even launched into my speech, she stopped me.

'Tressa, don't you go bringing up anything, you hear?' she warned. 'I don't want to talk about it. Any of it. D'you understand?'

I nodded, helpless. I felt so guilty then, looking at her scrawny frame, at the skinny wrists poking out from the arms of her dressing gown. It felt like it was my fault. If I hadn't insisted on having the baby, if I'd only listened to her and got the abortion, then none of this would have happened. Nobody would have found out about Jason, all the kids would still be living at my mum's and she wouldn't be the wreck she so clearly was now. I hadn't seen her in such a long time and I had no idea how bad things had got.

For the rest of the day, I cleared up round the house. I even went shopping and bought a bit of food to cook. I didn't know if Mum was pleased that I was there or not – she didn't seem to be bothered either way, but then she had taken a lot of drugs in the past few days and she was still very dopey. Alex and Vanessa turned up in the afternoon and before long everyone was in the kitchen, laughing and joking. Billy had started on his bottle of sherry at midday and by early evening he'd nearly drunk the lot. There was hash and booze, and eventually the kit came out.

I was offered some but vehemently refused. I hated kit. I hated what it had done to my family. There was a time before heroin had taken hold of my mother – a time when she had some hope, some control and some strength. But all that was long gone now. I saw in those first hours at her house that she was now a very serious addict. It had taken her family, her belongings and her looks, and now it was destroying her health.

'How long are you staying?' Mum asked that night.

'I don't know,' I said. 'I've got to go back to Dumfries.'

'Aye, but you don't have to go back right away, do you?' she said. 'You could stay here a while with us.'

That made me feel nice. Perhaps she'd missed me after all and she wanted me with her?

'Aye, I could stay a wee while,' I said. Despite all the drugs, the rubbish, the stink of urine, the dirty floors and filthy walls, I wanted to stay here with Mum. She was all I had left from my old life.

Over the next few days, I spoke to Adam and he agreed to bring the rest of my stuff round to my mum's house – my TV, jewellery and clothes. All the things I'd left at my dad's place when I walked out.

He seemed shy and embarrassed when he came round. I knew it was over between us but I was still shocked when he told me that Dad had said he could stay at his place. It was a real slap in the face – Dad wanted Adam but he didn't want me, his own daughter! I told him I didn't want to see him again.

That afternoon, I went through all my bags, checking to

make sure everything was there. It was only a one-bedroom flat so I had to sleep on the couch but at least now I had my nice duvet and fluffy pillow. It was weird, seeing all my nice clothes and belongings in this squalor. It seemed out of place.

Billy's room was the worst – he'd had a dog at one time, which had pooed and weed all over the floor. The dog was no longer around but the smell lingered on. Billy's bed was a bare mattress with a filthy duvet. Being a long-term alcoholic, he wet his bed most nights. The smell was so bad I couldn't go into their room at all.

Mum and Billy watched me and picked up some of my stuff, moaning about the fact that they didn't have any money for the rest of the week. I saw the hungry, desperate look in their eyes and I knew they were rattling. They went on and on until eventually I gave in.

'Here, you can take some of my stuff if you like,' I told them.

I knew what they were going to do – sell it to buy kit – but I didn't care. I wanted to help them out and it didn't matter to me. It was only stuff after all. I kept back some of my nicer clothes but I let them take the TV, my CD player, an old mobile phone that I didn't use anymore, some bracelets and a few other bits like perfume and handbags. They were grateful. I could see it was hard work to feed their habits every day – and Alex and Vanessa were now full-on addicts too, so between them they needed to get quite a bit of money.

A week into staying at my mum's, I phoned Helen. She sounded alarmed to hear that I'd moved into my mum's place but I reassured her that everything was fine and I was planning on coming back to Dumfries soon.

'The problem is that we don't have a place for you at Roselands anymore,' she said. 'And it won't be possible for you to find another placement like that because of your age. If you want to return to Dumfries, the only option is for us to find you a private let. Is that what you'd like?'

'Aye, that sounds fine,' I said. 'Once I'm back, I'll try and get my old job back and then, you know, just go on from there.'

There was a brief pause.

'I'm sorry it didn't work out with your dad, Tressa,' she said.

'Aye, me too,' I said.

'Okay, well, I'll start looking for a flat right away and I'll call you when I've found something. In the meantime, look after yourself, okay? We'll get you back to Dumfries in no time!'

A week later I was sitting in the living room with Mum, Billy, Alex, Vanessa and Alex's pal, David. They had managed to get a few bags of kit and were busy cooking up. Vanessa and Alex were sprawled out on the floor, already sparko, and she had big patches of sweat under her arms. I watched as Mum smoked hers off the foil. Then my eye caught Alex's – he'd been watching me the whole time, a strange half-smile on his lips.

'Hey, Tressa, you want to try some?' he asked.

'No,' I replied quickly. I wasn't interested in getting into kit like everyone else – I had seen how much damage it had caused my family.

But as one by one of them smoked it, I began to feel increasingly left out. It was like they were all part of the same gang and I was on the outside. *Oh, what harm would it do just to try?* I thought. I wanted to know what it was like. I wanted to see why they were all so into it.

This idea kept going round and round in my head and when Vanessa said to me ten minutes later: 'You should try some, Tressa,' I replied, 'Okay, I'll have a little line then.'

It was the biggest mistake of my life. The moment the opiate hit my bloodstream, I began to feel desperately sick. The next minute I knew I was in trouble and I scrambled to my feet. I hurled myself at the toilet just as the first retch took hold of me, and I threw up loudly and violently in the bowl. Again, it took hold and I threw up again. And again and again and again. I collapsed on the toilet floor, panting and breathless, streaks of vomit and dribble hanging off my mouth.

'Are you okay?' Mum called out from the living room. I couldn't even answer her back. I pushed myself up and vomited once again. I stayed like that for ages, just sitting down on the floor in between bursts of sickness. Of course, there was nothing left for me to throw up anymore so it was just bile coming out.

This went on all night long. Every time I tried to take a sip of water, it came back up again and all my skin started to feel itchy.

'You should have some more,' Vanessa said. I just stared at her, dumbfounded.

'How's that going to help?' I asked her in a thick voice.

'It will, trust me,' she said as she handed me the tooter. I took another drag and began to feel quite drowsy. She was right. The sickness started to ease a little, and I curled up on the sofa and eventually passed out. But I woke up feeling sick again the next day – again Vanessa said I should take some

217

more to stop it, so I did. A week passed and I had slipped into the habit of having a little every day with the group.

David and I were getting along very well by now but when the call came through from Helen, I was relieved to hear they'd found me a flat in Dumfries. I knew that it was time for me to leave my mum's place – I'd taken kit with them for a week and I could sense that if I didn't stop now, I'd end up with a habit just like the rest of them.

I packed my bags and waited for the taxi to take me to the train station. As I left, Mum shoved a bag of heroin in my rucksack.

'Just in case you fancy it,' she winked. Then she gave me a hug and I left.

At the station I dug out the little bag mum had given me and threw it in the bin. I wasn't going to take any more heroin. I knew it was no good for me and I knew that in Dumfries I could be free of all of that. I didn't know any addicts there and I wasn't going to start looking for a way to score. No, I'd tried to make it work with my dad and then my mum but I could see that it hadn't done me any good at all. My plan was to move into the private let and try to get my old job back. I longed for a cleaner life, a life free of all this mess. And I knew that as long as I could get back to Dumfries and stay there, I would be okay.

CHAPTER 21

Darren

I stretched out on the long, comfy couch and settled down for an evening of watching TV. This was a beautiful flat and the past two weeks had been blissful. My care workers had helped me to move into the one-bedroom apartment in the centre of Dumfries and from the moment I arrived, I loved it. It had white painted walls, pine floors and sturdy oak furniture. It was a really beautiful place and I realised I was lucky to get it. In the first week, I met up with all my old friends from school and even went round to the stables to see Jan. She was pleased to see me but I could tell she was wary – she knew all about my family and when I told her I'd been staying with my mum, she asked me outright if I'd taken any drugs.

'Aye, I did,' I told her. I didn't want to lie to her. 'But I'm not doing it any more. I've come back to get away from all of that. In fact, I was wondering if I could have my old job back.'

Jan was brushing down one of the horses and she carried on for a while, letting my question hang in the air.

I shifted nervously from one foot to the other.

At last she said, 'Why don't we give it a couple of weeks? I'd like to have you back, Tressa, but only if you're clean. I can't have you working around here with the children and the animals if you're on drugs.'

'Aye, all right,' I said. I was a little disappointed but I understood that she had to be sure.

'Come back in two weeks' time,' she said. 'And then we'll get you back to work. But only if you're clean.'

Next, I visited the country house hotel where I'd worked as a chambermaid to fill out an application to get my old job back. They seemed keen to get me back to work and assured me it would only take a week to sort out my application. In the meantime, I shopped, cooked for myself and spent a while arranging my furniture in the flat. It felt so good to be out of Billy's stinking, grubby doss house – and even better to be away from my family and all their dramas. As the days passed and heroin left my system, I began to feel more like my old self. I was also pleased to be able to hang on to my benefits at the end of every week rather than handing them straight over to Mum and Alex for drugs.

That evening I was planning on having an early night so I could get up early the next day and go to the pool for a swim. I was missing exercise. But at around 8pm the doorbell rang.

'Hey Tressa,' the voice came through on the intercom. 'It's David – let me in!'

I was surprised to be met at the door by David, Alex's friend. He was wearing a hopeful grin and carrying a large black rucksack. The moment he saw me, he turned back to the road to wave at an older couple sitting in a red Fiat with the engine running.

'It's okay!' he yelled in their direction. 'You can go now. She's here!' He gave them a brisk wave and the car moved away, then he pushed past me into the block of flats. I was too stunned to do anything about it.

'Who was that?' I asked him, closing the door behind me.

'Ma folks,' he said. 'They gave me a lift down here – I think they're quite pleased to see the back of me actually.' He laughed to himself and then looked around as we stood in the stairwell of the flats.

'So, which one is yours then?'

Reluctantly, I walked David up to my flat on the third floor. *What's he doing here?* I thought to myself as I climbed the stairs. *I didn't invite him! He's just turned up out of the blue.*

Once we were inside and David had dumped his bag on the floor, he gave me a big hug.

'It's great to see you Tressa!' he said, smiling still.

'Aye, it's nice to see you too,' I replied. 'What are you doing here?'

'Oh right! Yeah, well, I want to get clean. Just like you! I thought I'd never manage it up in Livingston so I thought I'd come down here to stay with you to get away from all of that.'

'Aye, well, you're not really meant to stay here, you know,' I said, turning away from him. 'My tenancy agreement says I can't have other people living here.'

I felt embarrassed and put out all at the same time – it's not like he even asked me! The thing was, at the end of my stay at Mum's house we'd snogged a couple of times and I guess this meant he thought there was something between us. I cursed myself then for being so weak. Why had I led him on? This was the last thing I wanted!

'Aye no bother,' he said, taking off his jacket and plonking himself down on my lovely sofa – the sofa where I'd just been lying moments before, happy and blissfully alone.

'I'll just kip down here a couple of weeks. You know, just until I get myself sorted out. That's all right, isn't it?'

I just nodded and went through to the kitchen to make a cup of tea.

An hour later David seemed restless – he kept flicking the channels on my TV, cursing the lack of any decent programmes.

Finally, exasperated, he switched the TV off altogether.

'So, are you going to show me about then?' he asked. It was 9pm and I'd hoped to be able to go to bed in an hour, but David obviously had other ideas.

'What – now?' I asked, hoping to put him off the idea of going out.

'Aye, why not?' He jumped up and put his coat back on. 'I've never been to this area before – I'd like to take a look.'

He was so keen to get out of the flat that I practically had to run down the stairs after him to keep up. Outside, it was pitch black and freezing cold, and my breath came out of my mouth in swirling clouds of condensation.

'I'll take you down the sands,' I told him. 'Come on – there's a big river and bridges and an island in the middle.'

As we walked, David brought me up-to-date on all the comings and goings with my mum, Billy, Alex and Vanessa. It was a depressing conversation – in truth, I'd been quite happy for the past fortnight, not having to listen to the list of my mother's many woes every day and night. We walked along the riverbank and David asked me about how I had ended up down here. I told him all about going off the rails and ending up in St Katherine's, and then I told him about the social workers putting me in Roselands to get me away from my family.

'It's been good for me, this place,' I told him as we walked. 'I passed some of my exams and I've been working at the stables and the hotel.'

'Ha!' David laughed to himself. 'I reckon my parents will be well chuffed I'm here now and not cluttering up their house with all my shit.'

'It was nice of them to give you a lift here,' I said. 'I mean, it's quite far.'

'I think they'd have dropped me in Tahiti if it meant I wasn't going home again!' he smiled. 'They've had enough. Can't blame them really – I've been on the kit for years. Lots of time in prison, stealing... You know, all that stuff. They gave me forty quid tonight – I think they're hoping that's the last they'll see of me for a while.'

We had reached the centre of town near the bridge by then and were sitting down on a park bench to watch the orange streetlights bounce off the black water in the river below. To our left were the public toilets where a handful of junkies stood around, blowing into their cupped hands to keep warm and smoking. David looked over at them and then quickly looked back to the river. His left leg jiggled up and down and then he leaned forward and put his hands on his knees. He puffed his cheeks out several times then swept his hair back from his head with his hands, hooked his fingers together and leaned back. I knew what was coming before he even said it.

'I could really do with a bag,' he muttered out of the corner of his mouth, as he stole a furtive look in my direction.

'I'm sorry, David,' I told him firmly. 'I don't know anyone here. I can't help you.'

'Yeah, but I could sort it,' he said, his eyes darting over to the public toilets. I knew I couldn't stop him; he had already made up his mind and the next thing I knew he was striding over to the group of men hanging around the loos. I watched him strike up a conversation but I didn't follow him. I didn't want to get involved in this. He was back on the bench within a minute.

'They said they couldn't get me anything.' He looked really annoyed and was hopping about from one foot to the other. 'It's because they don't know me. They don't trust me.'

'Let's just forget it, eh?' I suggested. 'It's getting late. We'll go back to the flat...'

'Nah, I know where to go!' he said, pulling me up by my arm.

'Where are you taking me?'

'Centre of town.'

'Why?'

'We've got to find a *Big Issue* seller. They'll sort us out.'

As it turned out, David was right. We found a Polish *Big Issue* seller outside McDonald's and he agreed to get some kit for David, as long as he sorted him out too. I tagged along behind as he took us to a house to score and then we went back to the guy's house to halve the bags.

I watched as the Polish guy got out some fresh tools and

started cooking up to inject. David asked the guy to do it to him, too.

'Here, you want some?' David asked me.

'Nah, you're all right.' I was nervous being in this stranger's house. In fact, I didn't really know either of them very well and I didn't want to get dragged into the kit again.

I sat watching as the bloke injected David. At first his face muscles relaxed and he lay back on the sofa, with his eyes closed, but a few seconds later his eyes sprang open and he clutched his arm in pain.

'Ow ow ow!' he growled.

'What is it?' I asked.

'Citrus burn!' he said, grimacing. 'Too much vitamin C in it.'

I could see there was a line like a white bubble going all the way up his arm and he clenched his teeth against the pain.

'I'm not doing that,' I said. 'No way.' It scared me – but after about half an hour, I began to feel jealous of them both as they lay back on the cushions on the floor, their eyes rolling back in their heads.

'OK,' I said. 'I'll have a little. But I'll smoke it off the foil. I'm not injecting.'

The moment the kit hit my bloodstream, the familiar wave of nausea swept over me, but in another second it was gone and replaced by the feeling of sinking down into the floor. I was so relaxed I could barely keep my eyes open, but I forced myself to stay focused. I didn't know these guys at all.

Half an hour later, we went back to the flat and chilled out in front of the TV. David and I kissed a little but we were both too high to do anything else. In the early hours of the morning I took myself to bed.

The next morning I woke up feeling angry with myself. *Why had I allowed myself to get dragged back into doing kit?* This wasn't what I was here for – I was meant to be getting away from all of that.

David was still asleep on the sofa when I came out of my room and went through to the kitchen to make breakfast. I tried to be as quiet as possible but at the same time I was annoyed he was here at all. He had arrived, uninvited, claiming he wanted to get clean and within an hour we'd gone out to score. It wasn't fair!

So when his mum called my house phone, I told her straight.

'He went out last night and bought kit,' I told her. 'I don't think he's here to get clean at all.'

'Are you joking? I gave him £40!' she yelled.

'Aye, that's what he used to get the stuff.' I wanted him out – I hoped that by telling his mum, she'd come and get him. But it didn't exactly work out that way.

'What the fuck did you tell my mother?' he screamed when he finally woke up. Apparently, she'd left him a series of angry text messages on his mobile.

'The truth,' I shrugged. 'I'm not going to lie to her. Why would I do that?'

'Why would you do that?' he parroted back to me in a nasty way. 'Why? Because it's none of her bloody business! That's why! I don't need you bloody interfering, shooting your mouth off to my mother. Do you understand? Don't fucking talk to her!'

'Yeah, sure,' I whispered. It was frightening. I didn't know this guy at all and I didn't know how far he would go.

Would he hit me? What had he been sent to prison for anyway?

I avoided him for the rest of the morning but by lunchtime he was keen to go back into town to buy some more stuff. I wanted to go shopping anyway so I walked with him to the high street.

'I've just got to pop into Superdrug,' I told him.

'Aye, no bother,' he replied. 'I'll come with you.'

I picked out the perfume I liked and my foundation and went to the counter. After I handed over my money, I went to leave. David had come up behind me but just as we got to the door, the security guard stopped us.

'Can you come with me please?' he asked, though it was less of a question and more like an order.

'Why?' I asked, confused. 'What's wrong?'

'I think your boyfriend knows,' he replied, looking directly at David.

I turned back to look at David and in that moment I realised what he'd been up to while I was shopping.

'Oh no!' I exclaimed. 'You didn't, did you?'

David shrugged as the guard led us through the back of the store to the office. He turned out his pockets and there were three packets of men's razors, a bottle of perfume and an electric toothbrush. The security guard said he was detaining David for theft and called the police – we were taken down the police station but when they realised that I hadn't done anything, they released me without charge.

'Don't worry!' David called out to me as I left. 'I'll be back home soon!'

Christ! What was I getting into? I thought as I walked back to the flat that afternoon. I prayed that the police would keep

David for a while and that he wouldn't come back to my flat. He said he'd be back home soon – whose home? This wasn't his home! He'd been nothing but trouble ever since he arrived and I just wanted him to stay away from me. But there wasn't much chance of that.

The next morning David was back at my door, grinning away.

'I met someone in the cells,' he said chirpily. 'His name's Darren. Say "hi Darren!"'

Right behind David there was a very tall and handsome man – for a moment I was speechless. Oh Christ, now there were two of them!

At least Darren had some manners. He actually asked me if he could stay for a few nights. I told him the same as David: he could only stay for a wee while because I wasn't technically meant to have houseguests according to my tenancy agreement.

Around mid-afternoon Darren invited David to go grafting with him, which meant stealing. And of course it didn't take long before they were back at my place with several bags of kit.

'What did you take?' I asked Darren out of curiosity.

'Computer games,' he said. 'They sell for a tenner each.'

So now I had two thieving drug addicts in my flat – two blokes who had made themselves very comfortable. I went outside and made a call to my friend Charlotte, who worked with me at the hotel.

'What should I do?' I asked her. I felt like they were taking over my flat. I was only sixteen and they were both much older than me. And bigger, too.

'Just chuck them out and don't let them back in again!' she said.

'It's not as simple as that,' I said. 'They'll smash my windows if I do that.'

'It's your name on the lease!' she warned. 'If you don't chuck them out, you'll be the one getting chucked out in the end.'

'Aye, well, maybe I can find another way.'

I went back home and by then the boys were cooking up and getting their arms ready to inject. When they offered me some, I smoked it off the foil. *I'll just do it this once*, I promised myself. *Then I won't have any more.* The rest of the night passed by in a dreamy haze and for a while it felt as though nothing mattered in the world at all. Everything was fine and everything would turn out okay in the end. *Just this once*, I told myself, *just this once today....*

But life didn't quite work out that way. For the next few weeks the three of us fell into a strange, new routine. We'd get up every day and then the boys would go out shoplifting. They'd come back in the afternoon and we'd all take kit together. David had started sleeping in my room – again, it wasn't like I'd offered this. We'd gone to bed one night and had sex, and then he'd just started coming in every night. There really wasn't much I could do to stop him. I was slightly scared of him – he had a vicious temper and when he was angry, he would really blow his top.

'You can't have people staying here,' my new social worker warned when she came round that week. The boys were out grafting.

'I'm not having anyone staying here,' I lied.

'Well, we've had complaints from your neighbours about guests staying here and making a lot of noise late at night.'

'That's not from this flat,' I said.

'I'm just warning you, Tressa,' she said pointedly. 'It's for your own good. If there are people staying here, you will lose your tenancy.'

I realised I had to do something. So when David's sister called up later that day, I told her that he was out shoplifting. She seemed shocked and extremely angry.

He came back that afternoon – by then Darren was staying at a hostel – and for a while everything was fine. But when I told him about the conversation I'd had with his sister, he went mad.

'Why are you telling my family what I'm getting up to?' he was flabbergasted.

'She asked me! I had no reason to lie,' I replied nonchalantly.

'Of course you fucking lie!' he screamed. 'Are you stupid or what?'

I wasn't – I just didn't particularly want him around anymore and I knew the only chance I had of getting him out for good was probably through his family.

'Don't call me stupid!' I yelled back, enraged. He'd forced his way into my life, made himself at home in my flat, got me back on to kit and now he was calling me stupid. I ran into the bedroom and started packing all his things up. Then I chucked them out of the door.

'You can fuck off out of my flat!' I told him.

'Ah come on,' he said, softening now. 'Don't do this, Tressa.'

'Go on, fuck off!' I yelled. He looked at me for a moment, still angry, but he could see I was serious.

'Fine!' he said as he grabbed his coat and walked out.

'And don't come back!' I screamed at his back.

I was relieved to see him striding out the front of the block of flats seconds later and hoped that he wouldn't be coming back. When I'd calmed down, I put the telly on and made myself a bowl of Coco Pops. I was halfway through eating them when I heard the key turning in the door. Why hadn't I taken his key away? I felt so stupid. I ran out to the hallway and before I'd even realised what I was doing, I flung the Coco Pops straight at him. Only it wasn't him: it was Darren.

'Urgh!' he yelled as the bowl hit him square in the chest. 'Tressa! What the fuck?'

'Oh, sorry, Darren,' I said when I realised my mistake. 'I thought you were David. We had a fight and I chucked him out.'

I started to giggle then – there were Coco Pops stuck all over him. He grinned too.

'Look funny, do I?' he smiled as he brushed the little brown rice puffs off his coat.

'Come into the kitchen,' I said. 'I'll clean you up.'

As we cleaned Darren's coat, jeans and shoes, I told him all about David and how he'd taken advantage of me. Darren seemed concerned.

'You're better off without him, you know,' he said, looking me directly in the eyes. At that moment I got a jolt in my stomach. He liked me! I had always found Darren attractive but I hadn't known until this moment that he liked me too.

'So, you want to come grafting with me?' he asked with a twinkle in his eye. I thought about it for a second – I'd never done anything like this before. I was reluctant. *What if I got caught?*

'You wouldn't have to do anything much,' he went on. 'Just hold the bag.'

'Aye, all right,' I said. I didn't see why not. I hadn't been back to the stables since David's arrival – there wasn't much point, as I'd been taking drugs. And although I'd been successful in getting a job at the hotel, I hadn't turned up on the first day because I had overslept after a night on kit. After that I was too embarrassed to go back. So I needed money somehow. *Oh well*, I shrugged inwardly, *in for a penny, in for a pound*. I was doing everything else by then so I didn't see why I shouldn't start shoplifting too.

As we approached Tesco's, Darren briefed me on exactly what would happen. He'd lined two Farmfoods bags with foil to stop the security tags setting off the alarms. All I had to do was hold the two bags open while he dropped in the computer games. Each bag could fit twelve games and each game was worth a tenner, which meant that if we pulled this off, we'd be £240 richer by the time we were done.

My hands were shaking and my heart was hammering like crazy as we walked into the large Tesco's in town. The store wasn't too crowded and we quickly found ourselves alone in the computer games aisles.

'Okay, stand in front of me,' Darren said quietly under his breath.

'What about the security camera?' I was alarmed, as I could clearly see the camera in front of me but Darren wasn't bothered.

'I'm tall,' he said. 'I've got my back to the camera so if you come close while I'm putting them in the bags, it won't be able to pick up what I'm doing.'

So I hid in front of him while he dropped twelve games into each bag – they all fell perfectly into place.

'Okay, let's go,' he said when he was done, and I followed him out of the store. I was so nervous I felt sick – but as I walked out the door, the blood pounding in my ears, nobody walked up to us to stop us.

We went on a little way up the road but as we turned the corner, I shoved the bags into Darren's hands and threw up on the pavement.

'Are you okay?' he asked in a tender voice, rubbing my back.

'I think so,' I panted, wiping the spittle from my mouth. 'It was the nerves.'

'Aye, it's a bit scary the first time,' he smiled. 'But it gets easier. Come on – let's go and sell them, then we can score.'

That night, as I lay on the floor, letting the kit take over my body and mind, I felt myself floating away to another world, a place where there were no worries and nothing could ever hurt me. I wondered if this was how my mum felt. *Is this what happens to her? Does she go to another place too?* Weirdly, taking kit made me feel closer to my mum. I could finally understand her; I could finally see things from her point of view.

It seemed like I couldn't go back to my old life now – too much had happened, my safe haven had been invaded and I had nowhere to go anymore. I realised I couldn't run away from the inevitable. It just wasn't meant to be. I was never going to have the perfect life I dreamed of; somehow trouble would always follow me around.

I could never truly escape it, no matter what I did, so why even try?

CHAPTER 22

A Heroin Addict

Why did I do it? Why did I take heroin?

Because it let me forget. While I was high, nothing in the world mattered, nothing at all. It was the ultimate escape. And I had a lot to escape from: the trauma of my early childhood, the abuse, the rape, the pregnancy, losing Annie... all of it. I didn't want to remember a single thing of my childhood so I took heroin every day. And once it had me in its grasp, it did not let go. Even after I started injecting, I never felt the same high again. It seemed my tolerance to the drug just seemed to go up and up and up, which meant I was always chasing that feeling. So Darren and I stole, sold the stuff, bought the bags, went home and got high. And the next day we did it all again. And the same the day after that. And on and on and on – always the same. It was a miserable, miserable life and I was deeply ashamed of myself. So I kept getting high to block out that feeling too.

Meanwhile, David had his revenge. He'd threatened to come and smash my place up so when I left the flat for a couple of days, he was as good as his word. I came back and found that the place had been trashed – the windows were broken, the sofa was all ripped up, my telly was smashed in and there was spray paint on the walls. I reported David to the police and went to stay at Roselands for a couple of days while the staff helped me to get the place sorted out. The police told me they were questioning David but it came to nothing. He denied it all.

By then I had a real habit and when I moved back into my flat, I let Darren come with me. I was dependent on him – I needed him for the shoplifting and the kit.

One night, after we'd got some stuff and taken a hit, we were sitting at the table in the living room and Darren took my hand.

'Tressa,' he started nervously. 'You know that I like you, don't you?'

I smiled at him.

'Aye, I do. And I like you too.'

'No, I mean, I really like you. Will you go out with me?'

I sighed then and looked away. 'I don't know, Darren. It's not been that long since David.'

'Fuck David!' he said softly; then he leaned over and kissed me. It was a soft, lingering kiss. A meaningful kiss. And for the first time in my life, it felt right.

After a while, Darren pulled away and he looked at me hard.

'Tressa, I love you.'

'You can't say that!' I laughed. 'You don't even know me.'

'Aye, I do know you and I've liked you ever since I first met you but I couldn't do anything about it. I've just been trying to keep myself to myself but now David's not here, well, I don't see why I can't tell you.'

We took it slowly. Darren was a real gentleman – he didn't rush me and for a while I kept him at arm's length. I was wary about jumping into another relationship, particularly after the previous disasters with Adam and David. But Darren was nothing like David – he was a gentle giant. He wouldn't dream of shouting at me, and he was always kind and considerate, making me cups of tea and giving me lovely hugs when I needed them. I didn't even need to ask. It was like he could tell what I was feeling. Gradually, I opened up about my past. I told him about Jason, Bernie and Pete. I told him about Annie and the hell I went through over losing my daughter. I told him about my mum and family – about how I'd tried all my life to help her, without success, and my guilt at having a child at twelve years old, which meant my mum lost all her kids.

Darren listened and sympathised when I told him how much I was missing Annie. Okay, so he was an addict but that didn't make him a bad person. Most of the people I knew were addicts. He was sweet and caring, the exact opposite of the boyfriends I'd known before. He wouldn't dream of forcing himself on me or making me do anything I didn't want to. Even when we went shoplifting, he said I could wait outside if it made me uncomfortable. Each night we disappeared into another world – a world where we were there, but not there. It was like I was dreaming of being someone different, somewhere different, and for that short while I was happy.

Three months after we got together Darren left early because my social workers were due at 10am and they weren't meant to know he was staying with me. I had got used to lying to everybody – that's what I had to do to survive. We had our meeting, and I spent the rest of the day clearing up the house and watching TV. I waited and waited but he never came back – by now I was rattling, desperate for a hit but also worried. Eventually, one of his pals came to my door.

'Darren's been lifted,' he said bluntly. 'He's in jail. He told me to come and tell you to go and see him in court in the morning.'

I was devastated. For the first time I'd found somebody I really cared about and now he was locked away.

The next morning I made sure I was up early to get to court. I sat in the public gallery, chewing my nails, as each case came before the judge. Finally, they brought Darren in. He looked tired and jittery when I saw him coming up from the cells. But he flashed a huge smile when he saw me. I listened, incredulous, as I heard the charges against him read out. And then I had to stifle a giggle. He'd been caught stealing a packet of Wagon Wheels and a carton of milk at Farmfoods! After all those trips to Tesco's and the thousands of pounds of computer games he'd nicked, he got done for a pack of Wagon Wheels. It was ridiculous. The judge, however, failed to see the funny side. Darren had been caught shoplifting several times before and now he was in for a custodial sentence. He was given six weeks.

'I won't be long,' Darren shouted to me as he was led back to the cells and I raised my hand to acknowledge what he'd said. I didn't want to shout out across the court.

I returned home that day feeling despondent. The life of a junkie had slowly crept up on me – the lies, the crime, constant rattling and shoplifting had all become part of the routine. The problem was that with Darren away, I was stuck. I wasn't going to shoplift on my own and I didn't consider for a moment that I could sell my body. So I did what I could – I called a couple of Darren's pals and they helped me out a little. Mainly, I just sweated and rattled. It was six weeks of hell. For days at a time, I lay on my bed, willing the hours to pass quicker. Sometimes Darren called but mostly he wrote me letters and I wrote back to him. Being apart for the first time made me realise how much I'd fallen for him and a week before he got out, I told him that I loved him. He wrote me a beautiful poem which I still have to this day.

As soon as he got out, Darren went straight out to score. He came back home with lots of drugs and it was a wonderful reunion. By that point, though, my landlord had had enough and I was asked to leave my flat. The social workers found me a unit in Lockerbie where I could stay and I went there, while Darren moved in with some friends. It was great in Lockerbie – for the first time in ages, I was looked after. There were cooked meals and clothes bought for me. After all, I was only sixteen and there was still a care plan in place for my welfare. The social workers were still really concerned – they knew by then that I was taking kit but there was nothing they could do to stop me. I went back and forth from Lockerbie to where Darren was staying and by then I needed two bags of kit a day to stop me rattling.

For the next few months we bounced around different houses, all the while trying to steal enough every day to feed our habits. Gradually, I started injecting and my drug-taking soared. I woke up each morning with cramp in my belly from the withdrawals. It was impossible just to get myself out of bed – every joint in my body ached and yet felt restless at the same time. I couldn't sit or lie still for a moment. Before long the cold sweats would start and then I'd feel really sick but I had nothing to bring up but bile. Occasionally, we managed to save a little bit of kit from the night before and that would hold us until we could get out to the shops.

Kit stole my appetite so I didn't eat. Sometimes we'd snack on a pack of crisps or some cake but we never had proper meals. As I was injecting into my arms, I had massive bruises all over them from where Darren had been squeezing to make my veins pop up. But every day it got harder and as the months passed, my veins started to collapse from injecting so much.

Eventually, we ended up in Alex and Vanessa's place in Livingston and since they also had habits, things got worse. By that point we needed £600 a day just to hold Darren and me so the shoplifting went through the roof. We hit TK Maxx, for the football tops mainly, and Boots for the perfume, aftershave and electrical goods. At Sainsbury's we would walk in, bold as you like, grab a trolley and fill it with 15 inch TVs, DVD players and Blue Ray DVDs. At B&Q we nicked hedge trimmers, lawnmowers, hammers, tools, stepladders, drills and whatever else we could fit in the trolley. We knew a girl who would buy it all from us and for that we could get enough kit to hold us. Sometimes we went out grafting three times a day, just to get enough kit to hold us all.

I even went back to the papers and sold a couple of stories about my relationship with Darren and how we were trying for a baby – just so that I could buy more kit. Of course, I didn't tell the papers the reason I needed the money. It was just a means to an end, a way to get cash. Nothing mattered anymore except my next hit. I did everything I could to get money and I suppose I never considered the consequences. That's what heroin does to you; it blocks out everything that matters in your life and replaces it with heroin. I didn't think in terms of days, weeks or months anymore – I lived hit to hit, hour to hour, minute to minute. And in the end, of course, it all caught up with me.

In July I lost my placement in Lockerbie and we ended up moving in with a friend and fellow addict, a girl called Marissa. I'd just been given a large payment by one of the newspapers so I was able to help her out with her bills and the shopping. I even bought paint and wallpaper to decorate the place. One morning we were sitting on the couch, just getting ready to inject, when Marissa suggested I inject into my groin. I'd never done that before so I was reluctant at first.

'It's better that way,' she insisted. 'You get the hit straight away.'

So I asked Marissa to do it but she kept missing and every time she stabbed me, the pain shot up my leg, making me cry out.

'I'll do it,' Darren offered. So I pulled my trousers down and he got me straight away. We had a cuddle and I fell backwards onto the sofa. At the time I didn't even notice that Marissa was holding her phone towards me.

Marissa went out that night – she said she was taking herself off to the hospital but we didn't really understand why. The next morning Darren and I got up at around 8am and I went through to the kitchen to make a cup of tea. It was then that my phone started ringing. I ignored it at first but then the 'pings' started. Who was calling and sending text messages this early? I was curious so I picked up my phone.

'Have u seen the paper?' said one.

'U r not going to be happy' read another.

My whole body went cold. At that moment I had a terrible feeling that my life was about to get a whole lot worse. I sent Darren out to get the *News of the World* and when he came back, his face was ashen.

'YOUNGEST MUM IS JUNKIE' the front-page headline screamed out. Underneath were the words: 'Gave birth aged 12. Injecting Heroin at 16.'

There, on the front – on the bloody front page – was a picture of me taken the day before, as I injected into my leg.

'Oh no!' I groaned. Now my mind raced – it must have been Marissa. That was why she had whipped her phone out the moment I injected! She had filmed the whole thing and then sold the story to the papers. I was shaking now and sat down on the floor, not knowing what to do.

'Oh my God, Darren, look what she's done to me!' I started to cry. 'Look what they're saying about me! Now I'll always be known as the country's youngest junkie mum!'

'Hey, hey,' Darren put his arms around me. 'It'll be all right. Don't worry. Let's have a hit, eh? And then we'll think about what to do.'

Darren and I locked ourselves in the bathroom to take a hit and we were just about to do it, when we heard loud banging on the front door. My heart started to race.

'Oh no!' I moaned. 'What now?'

We went to the front door and were met with a crowd of people – there must have been a dozen of them, and they all looked very angry. Gradually, as my eyes scanned the faces, I realised that these were all the neighbours who lived in the small close.

'You better leave,' said the grim-faced man leading the pack.

'Yeah, fuck off, you junkie!' screeched a woman behind him.

'We don't want your sort here!' an older lady said, jabbing her finger into my chest. At that point the whole crowd started to shout and jeer at us, and I felt very frightened.

'Quick, close the door,' I told Darren. He tried to slam it shut, but the man at the front had wedged his foot in the doorway and Darren couldn't close it.

'We want you out of here,' the man growled. 'Just pack your things and go.'

Luckily, Darren's height and strength meant that he was able to give the man a quick shove backwards, dislodging his foot and allowing us to shut the door quickly.

'Fuck! FUCK!' I screamed as I ran back into the lounge. By then we were both panicking and I wondered how the hell we were going to get out of the flat without getting battered. Even if we got out, where would we go? We had nowhere.

'What are we going to do, Darren?' I whimpered, pacing the floor. He stood in the middle of the living room, in complete shock.

'I don't know,' he said, shaking his head. 'We can't leave now. They'll rip us to pieces!'

'I know, I know. God, that Marissa! What a bitch!'

Then the doorbell rang.

'It's them again!' I yelled to Darren. 'Don't open it!'

'POLICE!' a voice shouted from behind the door. 'POLICE – OPEN UP!'

'We can't be sure it's really them,' I whispered to Darren. 'Check the spyhole first!' I was paranoid by now – what if the mob had decided to fool us just to get us to open up again?

'No, it's okay,' Darren called out from the door. 'It really is the police.'

As Darren let in two uniformed police officers, we could see that much of the crowd outside had fallen back to the corridor. Some were already disappearing down the stairwell. A few of the angrier ones, though, held their ground. The older police officer turned back to them as the door opened.

'I said you can leave now,' he stated firmly. 'Go on, go back to your homes. I won't tell you again.'

Finally, the last of the neighbours turned and left, grumbling and muttering under their breaths. Both officers strode in and asked us to confirm our names; the older one said that they had had a call from the tenant, Marissa, who claimed we had refused to leave her flat.

'The lying bitch!' I screeched. 'She never asked us to leave! She's just doing this so she doesn't have to face us. After what she did, I'm not bloody surprised. I can't wait to get my hands on that Marissa. And after all I did for her!'

'You won't be doing anything to Marissa,' the officer said sharply. 'This is all your own fault. You shouldn't have been so stupid to take a hit in front of a camera.'

'What?' I was dumbstruck. He'd obviously seen that day's paper and he knew what was going on. Still, I was shocked that he was so harsh.

'Well, imagine selling your story to the paper like that!' he went on.

'I didn't sell it!' I yelled. 'Why the hell would I sell a story like that?'

'Nevertheless,' the policeman went on, 'you took a hit in front of a camera. It wasn't a very clever move.'

I was outraged.

'Fuck this!' I stormed off. 'Come on, Darren. We're leaving.'

We managed to get into the unit at Lockerbie for a while but from the moment the article appeared in the paper, my life was over. People were shouting at me in the street, saying I shouldn't be allowed to have kids and that my daughter was better off without me. They threatened to batter me. It got so bad that I was afraid to leave the unit and eventually a friend said we could go and stay with her, away from all the people who knew me.

One night, I broke down. I'd had enough. I was so deeply ashamed of myself and the level I'd sunk to. Every morning I woke up and wondered what was the point of going on. I had no reason to live and I confided in Darren that I just wanted it to end.

'I'm sick of this,' I sobbed to Darren. 'This isn't a life. I just don't want to be around anymore. I don't want to wake up again and feel shit. And know that everyone out there hates me and wants me dead. I might as well do them a favour.'

'Don't talk like that!' Darren said, his eyes filling with tears. 'I can't go on without you.'

'So what are we going to do then?' I asked. 'Kill ourselves together?'

'NO!' he shouted. 'There's got to be a better way. There has to be some hope for us. I'm not ready to give up and I won't give up on you either.'

'Then there's only one thing we have left,' I sniffed. 'We'll have to try and come off the kit.'

Darren stayed silent. This was an important moment for us but I knew that I couldn't do this without him.

'I've tried before…' he started, quietly.

'Aye, well, you haven't tried it with me before,' I said. 'If we do this, we do it together. No fucking around. We don't have any choice now, Darren. I can't go on like this. If you don't do this with me, I won't make it.'

Darren took my hands then, his eyes brimming with tears.

'I swear, I'll do it with you,' he said vehemently. 'I won't let you down. Okay – let's do this.'

CHAPTER 23

Back to Reality

'I can't put you on methadone straight away,' Jen, the drug counsellor, told us frankly. It was the end of 2010 and we'd finally accepted the help that the social workers had been offering us for months: a referral to a drugs counsellor.

'You and Darren have to keep drug diaries first,' she went on. 'I need to know what you are taking and how much, so that we can get on the right doses of methadone. You also have to demonstrate you are committed to this programme. If you want to go forward with this, you'll have to keep your appointments. You'll have to truly commit yourself to coming off drugs.'

It was slow going at first – for the first two weeks we just kept our diaries. And to be brutally honest, I was ashamed when I showed mine to Jen. It didn't make for good reading.

'Right,' she said as she read through my diary. 'I think we'll start you on 25 mils to begin with…'

'Twenty-five?' I was amazed. This was a really small dose. 'What's 25 mils going to do?' I asked.

'Now, look, I know it's very low,' she said firmly. 'I know it's not going to hold you and I don't expect you to stop taking heroin straight away. But that's how it works. We put your dosage up every second day until you stabilise.'

She started Darren on 35 mils and at first we were still going out grafting most days to hold us. But steadily, as the methadone increased, the withdrawals died away. Eventually, after eight months, I was stable enough to stop taking heroin altogether.

I felt different; I was tired all the time, really dopey and I could barely get out of bed each morning. It was hard to find the motivation to get out of the house each day, and Darren and I became like zombies, just sitting in front of the TV all the time. I lost sensation physically and mentally, sinking into a terrible gloom.

Worse still, Darren and I didn't have anything to talk about. Our whole relationship had been built on drugs. Before, there had been excitement and activity as we went out every day shoplifting to feed our habits but now we had nothing to do and nothing to fill the vast, empty hours each day.

So we talked. We talked a lot about our lives before heroin – about the things that had led us down our destructive paths. I told Darren all about my childhood: about growing up in and out of care, my difficult relationship with my mum and the abuse from my brother. It was hard but it felt like I needed to start talking about these things. I'd spent too long bottling them up, trying to escape, and I needed to let it all come out. Darren, too, talked about his childhood and I learned so much more about him.

My head was clearer than it had been in years and now, lying in bed at night, I finally mourned for the little girl I'd lost. Some nights I wept for hours, clutching the caramel-coloured teddy bear that had once belonged to my beautiful daughter. I held it to my face and let the soft furry tufts brush along my cheek. I inhaled hard, trying to capture that magical scent of baby – but it was now long gone. I thought about how old she'd be now and what she would be doing. The adoptive parents sent me letters every six months, giving me updates on Annie's progress, and I read these over and over again. Each time, they broke my heart afresh.

The latest read:

Annie is physically very healthy, slightly above average height for her age and her weight is totally in proportion. She's up to date with all her vaccinations and has lovely teeth.

She's meeting all her developmental milestones beautifully. She appears very bright, can read numbers 0–9 and can count fluently to twenty. She can recognise many letters and can spell 'dog'. She's just learning to write her name. She loves playgroup and is now beginning to make little friendships.

She loves to play in the garden, play with her pets, bake, paint, make stuff, plant seeds and swim. She's had her first holiday abroad which was so enjoyable for her – she just swam and played all day.

In the simplest, age-appropriate terms, she knows that she's adopted. She has asked for your name on one occasion and we told her. She's a very happy, chatty, self-confident and together little girl. We will write again in six months.

With best wishes.

She knew my name! It was wonderful and completely depressing at the same time. I didn't know how to react to these letters. On the one hand, I yearned for news about my daughter – I was hungry for information, desperate to find out how she filled her days, what she loved to do, how far she had come in her development. On the other hand, every little revelation left me weak with sadness and an aching longing to hold her in my arms. I needed to feel her, I needed to see her. If I'd known the brutal, uncompromising pain of giving up my daughter – the daily struggle to put her out of my mind – I wondered if I would ever have chosen to do so.

Now that I was clean and my head was clear, Annie was with me all the time, at the very forefront of my thoughts. She never left me – wherever I was, whatever I was doing, I was simultaneously thinking about her. If I passed little girls in the street, I'd make quick mental calculations on how old they might be and then compare them in age to Annie. Some days I couldn't leave the house for fear that every girl I saw would remind me of her. I knew she didn't live in this part of the world anymore; I'd been told that. There was no chance of bumping into her whatsoever. Yet still, it didn't stop my imagination imprinting her face on all the children I saw in the street.

The rage and envy were also hard to cope with – they had given her a good life. I couldn't deny that – already she had been on her first foreign holiday. I could never have given her those sorts of opportunities. But what made them better than me? Nothing! Nothing except money! Because they had had better starts in life, better opportunities, they were wealthier and that, in the minds of everyone, made them better parents. It killed me to know that they had all the joys of being with my daughter – the playing, the swimming, the baking and painting – just because of their status in the world. It wasn't fair. None of it was fair and I felt that injustice so acutely sometimes that it was almost a physical pain, like a stab in the guts. It made me want to scream, to hit out, to smash the room to pieces. Yet there was nowhere for my rage to go – no place for this bubbling, boiling cauldron of anger. I just had to live with it.

But worse than any of this was the thought that one day Annie would grow up and read about me. She would read about how I'd turned to heroin at sixteen and she would realise that she had a junkie mother. And I couldn't bear it. I couldn't bear the thought that she would hate me for being a useless, worthless addict. That she would think she was better off without me. I wanted so much to turn my life around because I knew that one day she might come looking for me. I hoped she would, anyway. And I wanted her to be pleased with the person she found: the kind of mother who would make her proud.

There was so much I had to face up to in those months. In nearly two years of drug addiction, I'd been caught shoplifting more times than I could count and it meant I had to go to court. In the bad old days, I had just failed to turn up for my court appearances and that only made things worse – there were unpaid court fines and judgments against me for breach of bail. But I couldn't keep ducking my responsibilities: I had to take full account of my actions. It was terrifying – my lawyer said I shouldn't worry too much and that because of my age and background, it was unlikely I would be given a custodial sentence. Still, I couldn't help shaking with fear when I went before the magistrate's court. It all seemed so serious and formal. I felt small and helpless. Fortunately, I was only given a twelve-month probation order but it was still enough to make me weep with shame. I knew that from then on the criminal conviction would go against me in all aspects of my life. If I tried to get a job, it would be twice as hard.

And now that the heroin had stopped blocking out all my feelings and my fears, they returned tenfold to haunt me. During the day I would get panic attacks, seemingly for no reason. I could be walking along the street normally, when suddenly I'd be gripped by a crippling fear of something terrible happening. It was enough to make me stop dead, completely paralysed with terror. I didn't know what I was scared of exactly – or who – I just knew that my heart was racing like crazy and I was taking in huge lungfuls of air. During these attacks, all I wanted was to run away and hide. My eyes would scan my surroundings and if I could find a little doorway, I'd squeeze myself in and phone Darren from my mobile.

'Please come and get me,' I'd whisper into the phone, my hands hardly able to grip the handset as they were trembling so much. 'It's happening again. Please come and find me. I can't move.'

It would take at least three or four hours for the fear to subside, and even then only with the help of anti-anxiety drugs like Temazepam or Diazepam. The panic attacks became more frequent the more time went on and the closer it got to the date of Jason's release from jail. The nightmares and flashbacks also increased. Some nights I cried out so loudly, it scared Darren half to death. I'd talk, scream, cry and even fight in my sleep. He woke me once from a nightmare to tell me I'd been punching lumps out of him. I just looked at him with uncomprehending, bloodshot eyes and for a moment, I didn't know who he was.

It took several seconds before I was able to recognise him and then another minute before I could talk.

'I was back there again,' I explained hoarsely.

'Where? In the brickyard?'

Just the mention of the place made me break down, and Darren held and rocked me then, telling me that everything was okay and he would never let anyone hurt me again.

The only place where I felt any relief was in the peaceful surroundings of Polkemmet Country Park. We had settled in a flat in Bathgate and I could walk to the park in half an hour. It was only there, away from the traffic and the harsh, grey concrete of the city, that I could truly relax. As I walked along curved woodland paths, bending round trees and sidling up along little streams, I could feel my breathing slowing down and the sounds of the birds jabbering in the trees put a smile on my face. Out there, I wasn't judged. Among nature, I felt free from all the labels I'd acquired in my lifetime: I wasn't 'Britain's Youngest Mum', 'A Junkie', 'An Abused Schoolgirl', 'A Failed Mother'. I wasn't any of those things – I was just me. Tressa. And that, I realized, should be my starting point. I knew I needed to build myself up again.

So I'd take myself off for long walks – sometimes for hours at a time – through the country park, the golf course, the pine trees and the large, solid oaks. I'd marvel at the busy squirrels that sprang through the beds of autumn leaves, hard at work before the winter. I'd eye the stealthy foxes that sometimes darted in and out of the trees, only to disappear again in a whisper. On occasion, I took my sketchpad. It felt good to be drawing again – I'd spent so long telling myself I was worthless, no good and didn't deserve to live that it surprised and delighted me when I found I could make reasonably accurate portraits of the wildlife I observed. I was finding my confidence again, connecting with nature – just like I'd done at Roselands – and slowly, very slowly, I built myself back up.

One day, after a long roam around Polkemmet, I walked into the kitchen where Darren was making tea and blurted out: 'I want a baby.'

'Really?' he asked, his voice full of surprise. It was something we'd talked about previously but it hardly seemed possible before coming off heroin. Now that I had feelings again, now that I was a real person once more, I knew I needed someone to fill the gap that Annie had left inside me.

'I've got so much love to give a wee 'un,' I said to Darren. 'I want to give a child all that love. It feels like if I don't, I'll burst.'

'Aye, but are we ready?' he asked. 'I mean, we're only just on the methadone programme. We need time to get ourselves together a bit more.'

'I don't need any more time!' I said vehemently. 'I've grown up so much since Annie. And the thing is that I know I can do it right this time. I've changed.'

Darren took my hands and looked deep into my eyes. Very slowly, he said: 'You can't bring her back.'

'I know! I know that, Darren! But it feels right this time. Now we're stable and I know that I can't ever bring Annie back but I can still be a mum, a good mum! I can do it. I promise you.'

Darren took me in his arms and held me tightly.

'You really want this?' he whispered into my hair. I pulled my head back to look at him face to face.

'I really, really do,' I said.

'Okay,' he grinned. 'Let's start trying for a baby then.'

CHAPTER 24

A Death

'Where is she?' I asked Darren for the fourth time that day. It was a Saturday afternoon at the end of July and we'd made plans for Mum and Billy to come round for dinner. I'd made a big bowl of pasta for all of us and I was looking forward to talking to her about our exciting news – I was pregnant! It had taken a few months but eventually I'd fallen pregnant in early May, and Darren and I were thrilled. It was the kind of good news I needed, since Jason had been released from prison in March and for a while, things had been really rocky.

My family had made it clear before he even got out that they were prepared to support him after his release.

'I've got to do this,' Mum explained to me on the phone when I expressed my hurt that she was taking his side again.

'He's my son and he's got nothing left but family,' she concluded resolutely. I knew there was no point in arguing –

her mind was made up. It felt like a slap in the face, though. In the past two years Mum and I had worked hard to rebuild our fractured relationship. She too had come off the heroin and was on the methadone programme, and we were both struggling to adapt to our new lives. For a long time I resented her and the way she had behaved over the court case. It seemed like my feelings always came second.

'Jason's your golden boy!' I said to her one day. 'It doesn't matter how I feel or what he did – the fact is you've always loved him more than me.'

'Don't be so ridiculous!' Mum had shot back. 'I love yous both.'

'Aye, and you loved me so much you turned the whole family against me!' I'd retorted. 'I never got the support I needed. Not from you or from anyone else. It was like I was blamed for what he did to me.'

The arguments had ebbed and flowed, sometimes gaining momentum, sometimes running out of steam. In the end, we both got sick of returning to the same old bitter grievances and, though we never openly said it, there was an unspoken agreement to stop talking about it altogether. I knew I couldn't change the past so what was the point of raking over it again and again? No, I wanted to look towards the future now. I'd been getting on better with Mum recently and I wanted her to be involved with the new baby.

But Saturday came and went without any sign of Mum.

'Maybe her teeth are playing up again,' Darren shrugged that night. Mum had been to the dentist that week to have some rotten teeth taken out. She was always complaining about her teeth and it seemed a likely explanation. Still, I smarted that she hadn't even called or texted to cancel our arrangement.

After a long day on Sunday decorating our hallway, Darren and I sat down in the evening with some oven chips and sausages. We had just finished off our tea when I got a call on my mobile. It was Alex's number.

'Tressa!' There was a weird, strangled urgency in his voice, a tenseness I hadn't heard before. 'Tressa, somebody's just been taken out of your mum's house in a body bag.'

'What?' I felt my stomach drop. 'What are you talking about?'

'I don't know,' he garbled. 'I don't know. I tried to go round there and I couldn't get near because there was police everywhere. Then I saw a body bag being carried out of her house and somebody said that a woman had stabbed a guy in there. I think you better find out what's happened.'

I rang off quickly and dialled 999, my heart thudding hard in my chest. I gave them my mum's address and told them I was Tracey Tallons's daughter.

'Can you tell me what's going on please?' I begged. There was a long silence on the phone then as the operator put me on hold to check her computer.

'Okay, Tressa,' the operator finally returned. Her voice was calm and steady: 'I'm going to take your number now and give you a call back. Okay?'

At that point I knew that something terrible had definitely happened. I knew it; otherwise, she would have told me that everything was fine.

So I sat by my phone, willing it to ring. I got up, lit a fag and paced around, desperate for the woman with the calm voice to call me back. I wandered around the flat, put out my cigarette, sat down, checked my phone, stood up again and then lit another fag. The seconds seemed to drag by, as I checked the clock on my phone over and over again: 8.03pm. 8.04pm. 8.05pm. 8.06pm. Ten minutes after the call to 999, I felt so impatient and overwhelmed that I borrowed Darren's phone to call Alex, making sure to keep my line free.

'They said they couldn't tell me anything but they'll ring back,' I said.

'Right,' he said. 'Shall I come to your place?'

'Yeah, sure. Come on over.'

Half an hour later Alex was at my door – he told me he'd stolen his neighbour's van to get to me. Together, the three of us sat in the living room and talked about what could have happened.

'She's stabbed him,' Alex said confidently. He'd spent a lot of time with my mum and Billy in the last few years. Even before Jason was put away, he was always round our house and since my brother had gone to jail, they'd become closer than ever. I listened to the confidence in his voice as he went on: 'For sure, your mum's stabbed Billy. That's what it must be.'

He sounded so certain that I thought he might be right. But still no call came from 999. I kept getting Darren to ring the phone to check it was working, but of course his calls came through no problem.

By midnight we were all very tired and Alex said he was going to go home. He left the house and had just pulled away when we saw a police car pull up the drive and stop outside the house. I knew they had come to speak to me; I just knew it, so there was no surprise when two officers got out of the car and walked straight to our front door.

I had a funny feeling in the pit of my stomach when I went to answer the doorbell: a churning dread that made my arm tremble with fear. I saw my shaky fingers turn on the handle – they were white.

'Tressa Middleton?' the female officer asked. She had a terrible look on her face, a look I really didn't want to see. It was one of pity, sorrow.

'Yes,' I said, my voice barely a whisper.

'Can we come in please?'

I led them silently through to the living room and sat down automatically on the sofa.

'Tressa, we're sorry to have to inform you that your mother, Tracey Tallons, passed away in her sleep in the early hours of this morning. We're very sorry for your loss.'

'What? No!' I replied, shaking my head. 'No, there must be a mistake. It's not ma mum. Ma mum's not dead. Someone said it was Billy. That she stabbed Billy!'

The officer sighed and looked down.

'No, it's not Billy,' she said. 'There was no stabbing, Tressa. Your mother was suffering from acute and undiagnosed pneumonia. I'm sorry for your loss. If it's any consolation, she didn't suffer. She wasn't in any pain.'

But I couldn't take it in. I was crying now – but not tears of sadness – tears of frustration and disbelief. I couldn't believe what she was saying. How could my mum be dead? How was that possible?

They left shortly afterwards and I called Alex as soon as they were gone, knowing he could break the news to Jason.

The moment he answered the phone, I started to sob, unwilling to say the words. And at that moment he knew.

'Oh no, Tressa! Oh God, no!'

The next few days went by in a strange, unreal haze. It was like I had fallen out of my world and into an alternative reality. I tried to focus on things that I needed to do but it seemed that nothing was worthwhile. Alex told Jason about Mum and I broke the news to Dionne – probably the worst call I've ever had to make. Apart from that, I barely ate and I didn't sleep. I just sat on the couch as if in a daydream. I had had cramps in my stomach earlier in the week and spotting in my knickers. The cramps came back again – but I barely felt them. *This is a nightmare*, I just kept thinking. *I'm going to wake up at any minute*. I didn't think this could be happening to me, after everything else that had happened.

I never had a chance to tell her how much I loved her. I never had a chance to make things right with her. I thought back to all those arguments we'd had over Jason and felt ashamed for accusing her of treating him like her golden boy. How petty! How petty, stupid and selfish! All these years I'd worried about her, I'd feared her dying and now it had happened, it felt like I'd never had enough time. What about Jason? It was even worse for him – he had missed being with her for the past three years because of me! It was my fault that he'd had so little time with her.

Guilt ate away at me. Was it my fault she'd died so young? Had I put her in an early grave? With all that stress created by the pregnancy and then losing the children, I had made all her illnesses and addictions worse. I knew that others were thinking the same – one friend of hers said as much to my face. When my appointment with the midwife came round and I discovered that the cramps I'd suffered three days before Mum's death had been a miscarriage, I just nodded as if in agreement. The midwife looked at me strangely.

'Are you okay?' she asked. 'Do you need to see someone?'

'No, it's fine,' I said quickly. 'I'll be fine.'

It felt like it was meant to be. I didn't deserve that baby – I didn't deserve happiness.

'I want to help,' I told Alex on the phone that week. 'You know, with the funeral and everything.'

'Ah, erm… Tressa,' he stammered. 'I'm not sure about that. Jason doesn't want you to be involved. He doesn't want you coming at all, actually.'

I was dumbstruck. How could he be so cruel? She was my mother too!

'It's not up to him,' I told Alex defiantly. Now that Jason was out of prison, we didn't communicate directly – Alex was our go-between. 'There's no way I'm missing ma mother's funeral. You can tell that to Jason. He can't stop me going.'

I was hurt that my brother was so against me going to Mum's funeral – it felt like he was controlling me all over again. I knew it wasn't right. I would never let anything stop me from paying my respects to my mother. After all, she and I had talked about her death before – it was a subject she was happy to discuss, though it always made me feel uncomfortable.

'I don't want to be put in the ground,' she'd said on more than one occasion. 'I don't like the thought of being eaten by bugs. Yeah, I know you don't want to hear it but you better listen because when I'm gone, I'm relying on you to carry out what I want! It's going to be a cremation. Got it?'

It was like Mum always knew she was vulnerable. I waited for the call from Alex to let me know the date of the funeral but as days turned to weeks, I fretted.

'What's happening?' I asked him in mid-August. 'It's been nearly a month!'

'Your family hasn't got the money,' he admitted. 'Jason's doing his best – he's put about £500 down but the total cost is £2,000.'

'Right then, I'll make up the rest,' I told him resolutely. 'But you tell Jason from me that I will be at the funeral and so he better be prepared.'

I managed to sell a story to a magazine to help cover the rest of the costs and the money went straight to the funeral director's. The date was set for September. Three weeks beforehand, I went to the chapel of rest to say goodbye to her. In my bag was a letter I'd written, a letter penned in the long, dark hours of the night. In it, I told her how sorry I was for everything I put her through – I told her how much I loved her and asked her to look after us all, especially my daughter and my wee brothers.

I was nervous as hell when I went in – I'd never seen a dead body before, let alone the body of someone I cared deeply about. Darren was there, holding my hand as we walked in, but nothing could have prepared me for the smell. Oh God, it was awful. I nearly retched before I'd even seen her. Somehow I managed to push down the feelings of nausea and I steeled myself to approach the open coffin. The woman I saw in front of me looked nothing like my mother – I thought she might look peaceful, happy. But she didn't; she looked like a waxwork – a decaying, destroyed waxwork. Her cheeks were all shrunken in and the skin on her face had started to blacken with decomposition. I gasped, and stepped backwards, then felt instantly guilty at my own revulsion. I wanted to reach out to her, to show my love to her, but in truth I was scared. This wasn't my mum. Wherever my mum had gone, it wasn't here.

I dreaded Dionne turning up – just fifteen still, this would be so much harder for her. She arrived ten minutes later and I asked her if she was sure she wanted to see her. But she was determined and I understood. She too had been separated from our mum for long periods; she too needed closure – but still, I could read the fear on her face. She was shaking from the thought of looking at Mum's dead body.

I took her hand, trying to give her strength, but the moment she approached the coffin, Dionne's whole body stiffened and her face contorted in shock. In another second, she collapsed sobbing. We hugged then and I told her we should just say our goodbyes and leave. She pulled out the roses she had brought with her, and we each took one and tried to place them in her hands. But Mum's hands were frozen solid and it was difficult to get her fingers open to take the rose. In my confusion, I started to rub her hands, hoping to warm her up.

'What are you doing?' Dionne asked through her tears.

'I'm trying to warm her up,' I said.

'I don't think it will help,' she replied in a small voice and we looked at each other. In that moment, I was transported back in time, and we were just two helpless, lost little girls once more – girls who just wanted their mother.

Finally, the day of the funeral came round. It was a beautiful sunny day and I felt good as I pulled on the black top I'd chosen to match my black trousers. I'd never worn this top before but Mum had spotted it in my wardrobe months earlier and had gone mad over it. It was long and silky, draping down like a dress, with feathers around the bust and sparkly bits on the rest of it. She loved it so much she kept trying to borrow it – but I always refused her. It had been a present from Darren and I knew that if I ever lent it to my mum, the chances of getting it back again were practically zero. I'd tried to give it to Alex before the funeral and asked that Mum be dressed in it for the cremation but he'd said there was no point. Jason had put his foot down and I wasn't allowed to have any say in the funeral arrangements. He was happy enough to take my money to cover the costs of the funeral expenses but he didn't want me involved in any other way.

I was nervous as I walked into the crematorium – it was the first time I would see Jason in four years, since before he was sentenced. I'd rehearsed this moment in my head so many times and I'd talked to as many family members as I could beforehand, telling them I didn't want any problems and that I wouldn't be offended if they sat with Jason during the ceremony. This day was about Mum, not about the rest of us. I took my seat on one side of the aisle, Dionne holding one hand, Darren the other. I tried to smile when I saw my aunties and uncles but there was a strange, tense atmosphere in the room and though many came up to me to hug me, others steered well clear. It was as if I had a terrible contagious disease and they didn't want to come near me for fear of catching it.

When I saw the pallbearers coming in with Mum's coffin, I wanted to jump up and help them. There he was – Jason – my mum's eldest son, carrying our mother's coffin on his shoulders and he looked for all the world like a man in deep pain. I knew at that moment that I didn't hate him. I didn't hate him at all – I felt the same as him, the same keen loss – and all I wanted was to share his suffering, to hug him and tell him that I forgave him.

But I couldn't. I wasn't even allowed to get near him. The police were there to ensure there weren't any problems, particularly when it came to Jason's rules of probation. He was on the sex offenders' register now and that meant he couldn't be near anyone under eighteen. We all sat through the service in a state of shock and misery – Mum had just turned forty-one when she died. It was no age at all. All the asthma, chronic illnesses, and the drink and drugs had weakened her over the years. Yes, it was a kind death, a peaceful death. But it wasn't kind to any of us, the ones she left behind.

During the ceremony we sat divided into our respective camps: me, Dionne, my dad, Billy and Darren on one side, and the rest of the family on the other. I held Dionne's hand the whole way through as she sobbed uncontrollably. Then the final music started up and the coffin started to move on the conveyer belt. No! I wanted to jump up and stop it from moving towards the curtain. No! I wasn't ready! I didn't want to let her go. I knew that once the coffin had disappeared behind the curtain, that would be it. I bit hard on my bottom lip as silent tears rolled down my face. Gradually, the curtain swallowed up the coffin until we were all left staring at an empty space. I hadn't realised it at the time but I'd been holding my breath.

I let out a long sigh and then looked around me, blinking, hardly believing that I'd never see my mum again. At that moment, I felt lost, cut adrift. And then I caught Jason's eyes.

Sadness seeped out of him and I knew in that second that we shared one thought: *What do we do now?* I just wanted to go over and give him a cuddle and forget what had happened. I wanted my family back. I didn't want to be the cause of so much bitterness and resentment. But that was impossible.

When Dionne ran over to him after the service to give him a cuddle, he pushed her away angrily.

'Get away from me!' he hissed, his eyes darting up to the police officers standing at the back of the room. His face was distorted with real panic and fear. 'I could get took back to jail for this! Just get off!'

Dionne was heartbroken; she didn't understand that he couldn't be near her because she was only fifteen.

She hurried back to my side and, together, we went back to my house. She was still in residential care in Stirling but the social workers allowed her to come home with me because they saw we both needed each other for support. We weren't allowed to go to the wake because Jason was there. Back at home, Dionne fell apart.

'I don't know what's going to happen now,' she said. My heart went out to her – she had lost everyone, just like me. 'I don't want to go back to Stirling on my own.'

'Don't worry, Dionne,' I told her, just as I had years before when we were both children in care. 'I'm here for you. I won't leave you.'

So I begged the social workers to let me travel back to Stirling with her that night. I stayed in her room with her and for a very short while, it was like we had never been separated. We curled up together in her small bed, and I listened as her breathing slowed and she fell asleep next to me.

It was a week later that I saw my mum. She just appeared at the end of my bed in the early hours of the morning. I sat up, surprised, but pleased to see her.

'Are you okay, Mum?' I asked her. In fact, she looked better than she had in years. There was a nice plumpness to her cheeks; her skin was clear, eyes bright, and her hair healthy and shiny.

'Aye, I'm good,' she smiled. It made me so happy to see my mum again and I sat up talking to her for ages. I told her I was sorry she hadn't got to spend more time with Jason before she died.

'You're not to worry about it,' she said. 'You know that I love you. I've always loved you, Tressa.'

Tears sprang to my eyes then and I smiled. It was so good to see her.

From that day, Mum kept turning up in different places at all sorts of times of the day. I could just be sitting watching TV and she'd appear on the couch or I'd be in the kitchen and she'd come through the doorway. When Darren asked me who I was talking to, I told him.

'You're hallucinating,' he said, a scared look on his face.

'No! No, really, it's nice,' I tried to reassure him. 'Last night, after we had that fight, Mum told me you were right and she said I should apologise. She's helping me.'

But Darren just shook his head. 'I'm worried about you, Tressa,' he said. 'You're talking to yourself all the time.'

'I'm talking to Mum!' I insisted.

'No, Tressa,' he said gently. 'Your mum's dead. There's nobody there.'

I thought Darren was making a fuss over nothing. What

was wrong with Mum coming to see me once in a while? I didn't mind it a bit. But Darren insisted on telling my social worker and they took me into hospital to see a psychiatrist.

'Where is your mum now?' the woman asked.

'I don't know,' I replied thoughtfully. 'Do you know?'

'Yes, I know,' she said. 'But you tell me.'

'Well, she keeps turning up here, there and everywhere so I'm wondering: did she die or was it all a conspiracy theory?' I leaned in and whispered confidentially.

The doctors said I was experiencing a psychotic episode brought about by stress and grief. I listened, tired and fed up. I didn't want their diagnosis. This was my mum and I knew that whatever I was going through, whatever was happening, it was just part of my journey. I discharged myself after two days and went home with a bag of Valium to help ease the visions.

From then on, I stopped telling Darren when she visited – I didn't want him thinking I was crazy and I definitely didn't want to go back into hospital. Gradually, as the months went by, the visions faded. I missed her. It had been so nice to see her looking so well and I tried to take comfort from everything she told me. The guilt had lessened over time and everything she said made me think that in the end, I wasn't to blame. One day I woke up and realised that she had gone from my life forever; she was never coming back again. But I was okay with that. I had made my peace with her.

CHAPTER 25

Healing

On my way back from a meeting with my social worker one day, I passed a shop I'd never noticed before – the sign read 'The Stone Ring' and in the window were a selection of crystals, statues of angels, incense burners and beautiful jewellery crafted from gemstones. Something drew me inside and when I walked in, the atmosphere was very calm and peaceful. There was a light tinkling music playing in the background and the owner, a small woman with blonde hair, gave me a warm and welcoming smile.

I browsed for a while, looking carefully at all the statues – there were wolves, fairies, unicorns and witches. It was an Aladdin's cave and for a while I was lost in a strange, fantastical world. On my way out, I saw a notice on the door: 'The Moot. Meetings every second Tuesday of the month.'

For some reason I decided to write the number down and when I got home, I called it. A lady called Esme answered.

'What is a moot?' I asked.

'It's a meeting place for all those following a pagan, nature-based, magical or alternative spiritual path,' she explained. 'We run different seminars and workshops. You might be interested in the next one – it's on meditation. It doesn't matter if you're new to this. We welcome everybody.'

I had no idea what to expect when I went along that day. The meeting was held in a room above The Stone Ring and there was a small group of women of different ages. Esme led the meeting – she put on a CD, told us all to close our eyes and then talked us through a meditation exercise. The next thing I knew, I felt a calm, relaxed feeling sweeping over me. I'd never felt like this before – it was so good. The time flew by and it felt like only a second later that Esme was leading us out of our meditations. Afterwards, I felt so refreshed and relaxed. Esme asked us all to describe how the meditation affected us and I did my best to explain.

'It was like I'd gone to a better place inside myself,' I said. 'A space of acceptance and peace.'

I was keen to learn more and to try it at home so I bought a couple of CDs from the shop downstairs, which I put on that night when I went home. Now I listen to them and meditate every night. It has helped enormously with my nightmares and panic attacks, and has given me the ability to cope better with the ups and downs of my life. That's not to say that I have entirely overcome my past – I'm still processing everything that's happened to me and coming to terms with my troubled early years. I still get flashbacks and nightmares – there have been times I've woken up to find I've wet the bed in the middle of the night, and I still wake up crying occasionally or fighting.

But now, when I have a disturbed night, I put on my meditation CD and let the calming music relax me and take me to a more centred place.

I was awarded compensation for the abuse at the beginning of 2014 – a lot of money – but it is held in a trust account so that I can only take a certain amount a year. The majority of it is set aside for Annie. One day it might be useful to her. I think about her all the time still, and I look at her pictures most days. But I'm not in a rush to have another baby now – I know that Darren and I will have a child when the time is right. I've got to make sure I am healed first, before I can take on the responsibility of another human being.

All in all, I'm proud of myself and how far I have come. I'm proud of both of us really. We managed to come off drugs together to forge a new, clean life for ourselves. I still have my down days – there are times I don't want to leave the house and I avoid going to playgrounds because it hurts to watch other children playing. If I'm feeling low, just hearing their happy shouts makes my chest tighten and it feels like my heart is crumbling into little pieces all over again. I can't stop the tears and I try to get away, knowing that people will think I'm crazy. I'm twenty-one now; it has been ten years since I fell pregnant, and Annie is nine. It hurts knowing that she is out there somewhere, calling another person Mum. But I hope that one day she will come and find me, and together we can make peace with the past.

Mum's ashes sit on my shelf in my living room. I'm only keeping them safe until Jason comes out of prison – he got jailed again after a fight with his girlfriend. I don't hold any bad feelings for either him or my mum; I know that might sound strange but it is the only way I can live my life, with love and understanding in my heart. I had to forgive, in order to let myself become whole again. Whatever my mum did or didn't do, she was the only mother I had and I loved her. In her own way, she tried her best and though at times it wasn't enough, I know that she loved us all.

As for Jason, well, he's still my brother. It was like his defence lawyer said: he didn't have any boundaries at home, no guidance, and he too was just a child when the abuse started. If he had been brought up differently, I know for a fact that it would never have happened. Things weren't as black and white as the headlines made out – they never are. We were separated so long as children that when we were put back together again in the same house, he didn't recognise me as his sister. It was like his feelings got all mixed up and there was no one around to set him right.

As for Pete and Bernie – well, I don't forgive them. I can't. They weren't related to me, they were grown men and they knew what they were doing was wrong. I reported their abuse but the police say there isn't enough corroborating evidence to go ahead with a prosecution, which is infuriating. I don't see why they should get away with it just because nobody else has the guts to come forward. There is something wrong with the laws in a country which state that more than one person has to be abused for a prosecution to go ahead!

Dionne and I are still very close – she's at college now and has her own place. She is happy and settled, and that makes me so proud of her. I still see Alex and I've kept in touch with my dad. He's apologised for chucking me out that time when I went to stay with him and today he's grateful that we have a relationship. As for all my aunts, I still see them a lot. After we lost Mum, we all became close again. They tried their best for me through the years, and I know it hurt them to see Mum's slide into addiction and losing all the children.

Sadly, I'm not allowed to see Ollie or Kai, as they have their own lives now. I still miss them and hope that one day they'll want to come and find their real family, but for now I know it's best if their lives aren't too disrupted. I remember how confusing and difficult it was for me being in and out of care the whole time. Stability will give them a good start in life and I pray they are with good families who love them madly. I hope they'll remember my mum – for all her failings she adored her two youngest boys.

Overall, the hardest part of coming to terms with the past has been learning to accept that it wasn't my fault. I took on so much responsibility at such a young age; I felt I was to blame for the abuse. But a friend explained it to me in terms that I finally understood. When I told her about all the bribes I took from Pete and Bernie, she said, 'That doesn't mean anything. You were too young to be able to understand what was going on. Think of it this way: you can ask a dog if he wants to go to the opera and he might bark happily and wag his tail. But does that mean he's agreed to go to the opera? That he actually wants to go to the opera? No. He doesn't have a clue what you're talking about and you can bet he'll hate every minute. In the same way, you were too young to understand what you were agreeing to. A child of nine cannot agree to have sex. It is a grown-up thing. You weren't old enough to understand.'

This made sense to me. I don't blame myself anymore, though I can't help feeling remorse at the way everything turned out. I regret losing my daughter, I regret the fact that my brother went to jail and I feel immense sorrow when I think about those turbulent teenage years I lived through. I know it wasn't my fault and I can't change any of it. But it's sad, nonetheless.

Today, I try not to think about it too much. I want to build a positive future for Darren and me so that one day I hope, when she is old enough, Annie will come and find me. And find a mother to be proud of.

I'm trying. Every day I'm trying harder to be a better person, grow more, learn more and find a sense of my place in the world. I look back to what has happened in the past and the person I was, and I know that I have come far already. There is still a long way to go. But I'm here and I'm ready for the journey.

Acknowledgements

Firstly, I would like to thank Katy Weitz – if it wasn't for you, I wouldn't have had the opportunity of writing this book for Annie so thank you for everything you have done.

I would also like to thank our publishers, Blake, Andrew Lownie my literary agent and everyone who has worked on this book – it means so much to me that you all gave me this chance.

I would like to thank Annie's adopted parents for giving her the upbringing that I could not and making her into the person she is today – a very big and heartfelt thank you.

I would also like to thank all my workers for not giving up on me when I needed help the most. You didn't have to keep giving me all those chances, but you did and without all your amazing help I don't think I would have been able to get to where I am today – a very different place than before.

A very big thanks goes to Margaret Scullion and Laura Mitchell – without you both my life would not have been worth living. Even the times you were very strict with me – I know I needed it and it probably helped to shape me into the person I am today.

Thanks too to everyone else who has supported me through the years – it means a lot to know that people do care and want to help, so thank you.

Finally, words cannot even begin to express my gratitude to Darren – the person who has had faith in me, and given me care, love and understanding when I most needed them. I thank you from the bottom of my heart.